the middle

the middle

How the Quiet Majority Can Mend a Divided Nation

Patrick Payton

The Middle: How the Quiet Majority Can Mend a Divided Nation
Copyright © 2026 by Patrick Payton

All rights reserved. No part of this publication may be reproduced, stored in a retrieval system, or transmitted in any form by any means, electronic, mechanical, photocopy, recording, or otherwise, without the prior permission of the publisher, except as provided by USA copyright law.

No patent liability is assumed with respect to the use of the information contained herein. Although every precaution has been taken in the preparation of this book, the publisher and author assume no responsibility for errors or omissions. Neither is any liability assumed for damages resulting from the use of the information contained herein.

Unless otherwise noted, Scripture quotations are taken from the ESV® Bible (The Holy Bible, English Standard Version®). Copyright © 2001 by Crossway, a publishing ministry of Good News Publishers. All rights reserved.

Scripture quotations marked NIV are taken from the Holy Bible, New International Version®, NIV®. Copyright © 1973, 1978, 1984, 2011 by Biblica, Inc.® Used by permission of Zondervan. All rights reserved worldwide. www.zondervan.com. The "NIV" and "New International Version" are trademarks registered in the United States Patent and Trademark Office by Biblica, Inc.®

Scripture quotations marked NKJV are taken from the New King James Version®. Copyright © 1982 by Thomas Nelson. Used by permission. All rights reserved.

Published by Forefront Books, Nashville, Tennessee.
Distributed by Simon & Schuster.

Library of Congress Control Number: 2025926841

Print ISBN: 978-1-63763-494-3
E-book ISBN: 978-1-63763-495-0

Cover Design by George Stevens, G Sharp Design LLC
Interior Design by Mary Susan Oleson, Blu Design Concepts

Printed in the United States of America

26 27 28 29 30 31 RR4 10 9 8 7 6 5 4 3 2 1

To Cindy

*My soulmate,
warrior princess, and
fierce defender*

*Only because of you
and with you
have I come this far*

Contents

Introduction 9

1. The Middle: A Philosophy 13
2. Problem Solver 25
3. Never Read the Comments 39
4. An Unmitigated Mess 51
5. Tribal Instincts. 63
6. We're Not That Different....................................... 73
7. Losing the Core 85
8. Leaderless 101
9. Beans and Cornbread 113
10. Choose Service over Privilege 123
11. Conversation over Conflict.................................. 137
12. Humble History... 149
13. Curious Rather Than Right 161
14. Our Way over My Way... 171
15. Risky Liberty.. 183
16. Yes, It's Love.. 193
17. Get in the Game 203

Acknowledgments 217

Notes 221

Introduction

> Everything is changing.
> People are taking their comedians seriously
> and the politicians as a joke.
>
> —Will Rogers

In the heart of America's political system lies the Middle—a growing group of people who sometimes wonder if they are the ones out of touch with reality, not for their sensible views, but because of the relentless shouting from the extremes around them. They question what happened to the great country that, not so long ago, prided itself on talking things through, rolling up its sleeves, working things out, and finding a better path forward together.

The Middle has grown tired of the incessant "us versus them" mentality that dominates nearly every facet of American life—religion, politics, economics, health care, climate change, abortion, race, and virtually every other societal issue in between. They are fed up with

Introduction

both sides of the political spectrum claiming to be right—and the other wrong—and using God Almighty to support their arguments, while failing to act in a way that reflects the good Word. They are disenchanted with the rigid litmus tests applied to nearly every issue—from immigration and gun laws to abortion, same-sex marriage, and taxes—tests that leave no room for discussion or middle ground.

Those Americans in the Middle want reassurance that they are not alone in this endless echo chamber and that there are others out there who want to make meaningful changes to bring compromise, civility, and less partisanship to politics and our everyday lives. They want to go to work, raise their children, build a future, and pay their taxes without unnecessary government interference. They want to pursue the Founding Fathers' promise of life, liberty, and the pursuit of happiness on their own.

Today, people in the Middle are tired of the government's overreach—deciding what kind of car they drive, the appliances they use, the schools their children attend, their personal and reproductive choices, their financial retirement plans, and even the news and social media they consume.

This isn't a political statement; it's a statement of fact. As the nation's population has grown, local, state, and federal governments have expanded in size and extended their reach deeper into the fabric of Main Street. This group in the Middle doesn't despise government, but they do resent the systems and structures of government that have locked us into endless left-versus-right battles and have turned neighbor against neighbor.

More than anything, those in the Middle want to be left alone.

Introduction

They recognize the government's legitimate role in society but are fed up with the "nanny state" mentality of local, state, and national politicians who seem to believe they know what's best for everyone and want to make every important decision in their lives.

They are sick of the zero-sum game of politics, in which elected officials and faith leaders claim the moral high ground on complex issues, leaving no room for compromise or mutual understanding. They're tired of the narrative that demands all or nothing. The Middle is weary of every issue being a choice between good and evil with nothing in between. Americans in the Middle want a political environment in which common sense, civility, and respect prevail; where differences and the complexities of life are acknowledged and understood; and where solutions are discovered through cooperation and compromise.

The idea of the Middle—and what we can do as a society to bring people back from the extremes —stems from more than three and a half decades of my experience with people in the pews (as a business leader), the pulpit (as pastor), and politics (as mayor).

Over the past thirty years, I have spent my life speaking to and leading people. This leadership has placed me before audiences ranging from thousands of weekly parishioners and various conferences to the United Nations, peace missions to Northern Sudan, political rallies, the chambers of the Texas legislature, and countless boardrooms—not to mention the living rooms of parishioners and one-on-one conversations with constituents and everyday clients navigating difficult situations. In all these settings, I have listened carefully, honored the humanity of every person involved, and tried

Introduction

to find a way to cut through the noise and reveal the heart of the unique challenges people from all walks of life face.

Now, with a humble heart, I'm ready to tackle one of the most serious issues in America today—and hopefully, with your help, to bring our country back from the extremes. Perhaps together we can begin a grassroots movement away from the divisive edges and toward the shared humanity and commitment to life, liberty, and pursuit of happiness that belong to all of us.

CHAPTER 1

The Middle: A Philosophy

The Middle is not a new concept. Dwight D. Eisenhower, a five-star general in the United States Army and later the thirty-fourth president, was a centrist and moderate who sought a "middle way" from the radicals on the left and reactionaries on the right. While most of his fellow Republicans at the time were committed to limited government, a capitalist system, and individual freedom, Eisenhower believed the federal government needed to be involved in its citizens' lives—but only to a certain extent.

On August 20, 1952, during a presidential campaign speech in Boise, Idaho, Eisenhower told the audience that the Founding Fathers had envisioned a government guided by a middle way:

> You see, there are many in our country who say there are only two roads to the future—one off to the right, by

following which we become reactionaries. We go back to the place where we think we should have lived in 1852. Then there are others who say you must continually go to the left. Those people say, "Let the government do it—turn it over to Washington." They go so far to the left that we call them radicals.[1]

Having served as supreme commander of the Allied forces during World War II, Eisenhower chose his words carefully in warning those in the crowd that going too far down either road could result in tyranny. He often compared American politics to bowling, referring to the extremes on both sides as the "gutters."

When Eisenhower initially ran for the Republican nomination for president in 1952, he did so partly out of a desire to prevent Senator Robert A. Taft of Ohio from getting the party nod. Taft, known as "Mr. Republican," was a staunch conservative, isolationist, and anti-Communist, who favored limited government and opposed labor unions and US involvement in foreign conflicts. Ike defeated Taft at the Republican National Convention in Chicago and chose California Senator Richard Nixon as his running mate.

Eisenhower admired former US Presidents Abraham Lincoln and Theodore Roosevelt for being men of the Middle. He respected Lincoln's methodical approach to ending slavery in America, while ignoring others' advice to do it faster because of his fear of losing border states.

Ike also celebrated Lincoln's ability to find common ground while passing the Homestead Act during the Civil War. While powerful groups in Washington, DC, wished to place the lands of the American West into the hands of a powerful (and rich) collection of men, others wanted the federal government to control the land and its natural resources.

Instead, by signing the Homestead Act into law on May 20, 1862, Lincoln allowed American citizens to claim 160 acres of federal land in the West if they occupied the land for at least five years and made improvements. It led to the greatest expansion in American history.

Ike revered Roosevelt, the twenty-sixth president from 1901 to 1909, for his ability to break up monopolies and regulate big business. Roosevelt enforced the Sherman Antitrust Act, dismantling powerful monopolies such as the railroad controlled by J. P. Morgan and James J. Hill, John D. Rockefeller's Standard Oil, and the American Tobacco Company.

However, Roosevelt's "Square Deal" didn't entirely destroy those monopolies. Instead, the federal government aimed at finding middle ground by balancing the interests of businesses, workers, and consumers by making large corporations conform to laws so they couldn't "exert undue influence and power over the people."[2]

Roosevelt "chose the middle way and we will always remember him forever because of that," Eisenhower told the crowd in Boise, Idaho.[3]

As part of his presidential campaign, Eisenhower implored voters to accept what he called "social gains": education for their children, decent housing, workers' rights, insurance against disasters and unemployment, and equal opportunities for everyone, regardless of race, religion, or national origin.

Eisenhower called those social gains "a solid floor that keeps all of us from falling into the pit of disaster."[4] He decried a federal government that was too big and did everything "but come in and wash the dishes."[5]

"But on top of that floor, let's not interfere with the incentive, the ambition, the right of any of you to build the most glorious structure on top of that floor that you can imagine," Eisenhower said. "We are going to gain those things by going right down the middle of the road that gives you every opportunity to expand yourself, to earn and save yourself and your family. We must go forward."[6]

On November 4, 1952, Eisenhower defeated Illinois Democratic Governor Adlai Stevenson II in a landslide victory, receiving 54.9 percent of the popular vote.[7] Ike was the first Republican president elected in twenty years. Four years later, he beat Stevenson soundly again, collecting 57.4 percent of the vote.[8]

During his eight years in the White House, Eisenhower had an average approval rating of about 65 percent.[9] He ended America's involvement in the unpopular Korean War, signed the first civil rights legislation since Reconstruction, championed the Interstate Highway System, worked to contain Communism, and balanced the budget three times, even while expanding Social Security.

By trying to find the middle way—even while facing opposition from some powerful people in his own party—Eisenhower's approval rating was higher in his final year in office than it was in his first.

The Middle: A Philosophy

After Eisenhower left the White House, the Republican party shifted away from his moderate approach, adopting a more conservative platform that emphasized limited government involvement in the economy, accentuated states' rights, and restored law and order during the turbulent 1960s. By the time Ronald Reagan became president in 1981, Republicans had fully embraced economic conservatism, such as tax cuts and supply-side economics—along with a range of social issues, from pro-life platforms to issues surrounding LGBT debates.

In recent years, American politics has moved further to the left under Democratic Presidents Barack Obama and Joe Biden, and further to the right under Donald Trump. This has left those in the Middle often feeling ignored and unrepresented.

When did the Middle become a bad thing? The last time I checked, being "right down the middle" has almost always been a good thing.

Golf is one of my favorite hobbies. The players who have the lowest handicaps are usually the ones who hit their tee shots down the middle of fairways and find the middle of clubfaces. Hitting a ball too far to the right or left can spoil the round of a lifetime, but figuring out how to hit every shot down the middle can transform an average golfer into a low handicapper.

Football—especially college football—is my favorite sport to watch. Teams that run the ball down the middle of the field typically score. Kickers try to find the middle of the uprights on field goals and extra points. No one gets bonus points for bouncing a ball off an upright.

The Middle

As Eisenhower noted, America's Founding Fathers hoped to establish a "middle way of government." In the closing of the Declaration of Independence, great men such as George Washington, Thomas Jefferson, John Adams, James Madison, and others promised to "pledge to each other our Lives, our Fortunes and our sacred Honor."[10]

These founders believed so deeply in the principles and cause of the American Revolution that they pledged themselves to one another. Men who debated and argued with great respect over significant matters—those who would go on to establish the greatest nation on earth—still found within themselves, despite their differences and disagreements, a purpose greater than their own ambitions. They resolved that the cause of the Middle, standing against the tyranny of extremes, was worth dedicating their lives to.

Our time in America is not much different, but something in our collective humanity—among our neighbors and leaders alike—has dramatically changed. Somehow, we have lost sight of the greater bond that unites us and brings out the best in ourselves during our most challenging seasons.

We find ourselves living in a time where the tyranny of the noisy extremes is turning Americans against one another on multiple fronts. We define ourselves increasingly by political affiliation, race, and identity, to the extent that we have forgotten what it means to uphold the sacred honor we owe not only to ourselves but also to one another as fellow human beings—and as fellow Americans.

It's time for the majority in the Middle to recover their voice and drown out the noisy minority of extremes that seek to control and divide. It's time for the Middle to reclaim the honor we owe one another, showing respect even when we disagree. It's time for the Middle to resolve to seek to understand other viewpoints and ideas before demanding acquiescence to one viewpoint loudly proclaimed by an extremist tribe.

It's time for the Middle to honor the complexity of difficult issues and to choose respect and integrity over vilification and demonization. It's time for the Middle to extend unlimited liability (love) to one another in the understanding that we all fall short, none of us is perfect, and the best we can hope to do is find our common ground and press on together. It's time for the Middle to recover its voice—rooted in the founding of this country—and reject the tyranny of the noisy minority.

It's time for the Middle to engage the public square—whether at the water cooler or in the bleachers of Little League games—and demonstrate what open minds and hearts look and act like in the true spirit of life, liberty, and the pursuit of happiness.

We are living in a political and cultural time defined by the old Pareto Principle, commonly known as the 80/20 rule. Today, 20 percent of the American population—10 percent on the far left and 10 percent on the far right—accounts for 80 percent of the noise that dominates air waves, debates, and political discussions.

Sadly, the reality is that the 80 percent in the Middle has lost sight of its power, voice, and solidarity. Yet if properly led and channeled, however, these strengths could embolden the Middle to drown out the noise from the 20 percent on the far edges—and, in doing so, save American politics and America itself from the tyranny

The Middle

of the extremes.

A nation divided right down the middle in the most recent US presidential election is proof of this concept, especially when working with a Congress that at any given time can barely eke out a majority. As bad as that might seem on the surface, it is less a sign of a hopelessly divided nation and more an indication of a country fluctuating along the Middle.

The Middle is all around us, yet the obvious signs are often missed. Its power is like a set of jumper cables—harnessing the best of a positive post and a negative post to create an entirely new source of power.

The Middle is like the mass of the earth—most alive and creative *between* the poles, and most deadly *at* the poles. No one lives at the poles for anything other than exploration and scientific discovery, yet between them the power of nature produces creativity, life, and activity, offering endless options.

As I found myself floating down a river, one weekend not too long ago, I thought about the complex journey of the Middle. Though occasionally it is good to find a brief respite on the shore, it is not where opportunity and discovery occur.

Depending on the size, depth, and speed of a river, the most prized fish—trout, bass, pike, muskellunge, and others—are found in the mid-channel. This is because food sources like mayflies, caddis flies, freshwater shrimp, and crayfish are located in the main current. Herons, egrets, ducks, and geese are often found floating and feeding on smaller fish or aquatic plants in the middle of a river as well.

The Middle: A Philosophy

Think about it: We are told to keep it in the middle of the lane when driving down the road. When we hang a picture on the wall, we'll sometimes use a measuring stick to find the middle and a level—with the bubble in the middle—to get the frame perfectly straight.

Most of us are living in the Middle right now and might not even realize it. Our homes are most comfortable with temperatures "in the middle," not too hot or too cold. We moderate the temperature in our cars and trucks for the same reason. We freeze our ice cream and heat our dinners, only to let it sit out for a minute or two until it's "not too hot" or "not too cold" before eating it.

Living in the Middle means striving for balance and moderation in our lifestyle—avoiding excessive alcohol, sugar, and red meat. It means not being too strict or lenient when it comes to raising our children. It also means being prudent in our investments, building a balanced portfolio of stocks and bonds without going all in on one strategy.

Most of us spend each day with our loved ones in the Middle. The typical day is filled with neither Valentine's romance nor unbearable tension; instead, we hope for a good day that isn't too high or too low, so our adrenaline doesn't spike. We simply "do life" with the people who matter most to us. This isn't settling—it's a safe and comfortable place to not only survive but also thrive.

Loud and boisterous extremes in America have been made *louder* and even *more boisterous* by the ubiquitous presence of the Internet and social media. Deafening voices on both the left and the right label and blame one another rather than seeking to understand the other side. Their struggle has become one of "us versus them," manipulated by the extreme 20 percent on the edges, who criticizes anyone who doubts, questions, or resists their chosen orthodoxy of the extremes.

Much like the Founding Fathers, who stood against the tyranny of a colonial power seeking to impose taxation without representation and erode America's freedoms, today's extremes are fueled by the same idea that everyday people must be told what to do, how to do it, and to listen to and follow only the voices of the powerful leaders of the extremes. Those on the extreme right and left vie for control of the agenda and lives of people because, deep down, they don't believe the average person in the Middle is capable of self-governance toward a sufficient pursuit of life, liberty, and happiness.

Partisanship and sometimes-aggressive division mark American history. But this partisanship has become overly personal, and division is treated as a badge of honor rather than a chasm to bridge for the good of us all.

The Middle is not a movement of people throwing up their hands and saying, "Can't we all just get along?" It is not a majority of Americans without backbone or conviction. This Middle is tired of sitting quietly while the noise of the extremes gets louder with each passing day. They are ready to rock the boat—they just need to know that this quiet majority does exist and they will not be alone when they finally raise their voice.

The Middle has witnessed the damage inflicted by the extremes for far too long and understands there is a better path for our shared humanity and country. It chooses not to focus solely on the positives and negatives created by either side but to embrace the best of our collective whole and what we can all bring to the better synergy of a new way.

Within the pages of this book, the Middle will find they are not alone in what they are hearing and feeling. The hope of this book is for the Middle to hear the calling that they are not the "crazy" or the marginalized but are instead the majority who must find their collective voice that has been drowned out by the very loud extremes. There is a stirring among the silent majority that is quietly echoing throughout this nation, waiting for a spark to ignite the flame of fearlessness to heal a divided nation. This is a calling of the quiet majority, not ignored, and one that will not come from the current halls of power. It will be a movement, once again, "of the people, by the people, and for the people."

CHAPTER 2

Problem Solver

Growing up in Oklahoma, I was exposed to the seductive certainty of extreme perspectives, after my mother, sister, and I found refuge among Southern Baptists amid the raging storm of our broken home.

I didn't start attending church regularly until after my parents divorced in the late 1970s. There, I was introduced to the "Moral Majority"—and its extremes. In the Southern Baptist Church, smoking, drinking, and cursing were forbidden. This extreme easily categorized people based on their life choices and seemed so sure and powerful. Who were we to question this authority and this segregation? After all, they were the expert shepherds, and we were just the lowly sheep.

I didn't realize it at the time, but one of the signs of extremism is a rigid certainty and a readiness to pass judgment on others—and to base it on some perceived divine or governmental authority.

We found safety and a supportive community in the church. Whether we realized it at the time or not, we were learning that leaders were not to be questioned. After all, they appeared to have their lives together, and it seemed to be working. But oddly enough, I noticed how certain people were viewed differently by those in positions of perceived power. Those in positions of authority seemed to have a difficult time understanding that many in the pews had imperfect backgrounds, yet they were still people who shared a common humanity and lives filled with stories we could all learn from with great humility and empathy.

It wasn't long before I realized that the men and women who were divorced, including my mother, sat in the back of the auditorium during church services. They were people who had done "those things." Failing to make their marriages work, no matter how hard they might have tried, came with a scarlet letter of "former this" or "former that." Rarely were they referred to as simply Mr. Smith or Mrs. Jones at church functions; instead, they were often seen through the lens of their mistakes and struggles. It was a kind of hypocrisy I was too young to understand.

In that Southern Baptist church in the 1970s, there was not as much of a shared humanity as a measured attainment of grace, righteousness, and standing. That is, it wasn't so much an attitude of "all have sinned and fallen short of the glory of God"[11] but rather one of "you've fallen much shorter of the glory of God than I have."

To be clear, I don't think it was done as a form of strict

segregation or labeling. I believe the hearts and minds of most of those in this large church were in the right place, but the seeds of "us versus them" had been planted. Over time, people in the church who didn't agree with you were overlooked and disrespected.

The social exclusion of people who had been divorced or had different views from the leaders eventually grew into the separation of the church and others—not just church and state. There was the extreme example of "churchgoing" people and those who did not attend church, who were oftentimes labeled as "those people" or in today's more common term, "the unchurched."

I didn't notice this dynamic until later in life, during my own season away from church. Only then did I personally experience the "us versus them" mentality. It wasn't a separation left up to the Lord of the heavens, who would one day divide the heavenly sheep from the goats, but rather an earthly action produced by faulty humans who segregated insiders and outsiders to the detriment of both. Those people who fell in the Middle—many of whom were trying to find their way and might even have listened to calm, gentle voices—instead became isolated, victims of the extremes operating inside and outside the church.

In the early 1990s, I led a Bible study at our church in Oklahoma with my wife, Cindy—my junior-high sweetheart. During one session, while reading Henry T. Blackaby, Richard Blackaby, and Claude V. King's *Experiencing God*, I asked, "Would you sell everything and just take off and see what God would do?" A few nights later at dinner, I told Cindy, "Maybe that's what we should do."

The Middle

We sold nearly everything we owned, loaded up our two young kids, and moved to Louisville, Kentucky, where I attended the Southern Baptist Theological Seminary. I didn't necessarily move to Louisville to become a minister; I wanted to prove a personal theological point—that God could be trusted if you left everything behind and trusted Him for the next step and everything in between. I left a well-paying job in the food industry and took jobs at a local Chili's restaurant and a tennis pro shop to support our growing family. Our third child was on the way soon after we arrived in Kentucky.

In some ways, this journey was my own personal experiment. But it was mine alone, and I didn't measure anyone else by where they were compared to where I was headed.

After finishing seminary, I didn't send out résumés for church positions. Instead, I waited, prayed, and watched for the next step, until I received a phone call from a group wanting to start a small church in Midland, Texas. This was on the heels of the Southern Baptist Convention's "Battle for the Bible," a ten-year conflict where the religious right and Bible literalists sought control of the largest Protestant denomination in the United States.

The "Battle for the Bible" was its own form of religious extremism, waged between the right and left sides of the Southern Baptist Convention. It became clear to those in the Middle that the church was no longer a place for discussion, debate, or differences. The people working in the extremes ostracized anyone who disagreed with them, in the name of guarding the truth once and for all. In the end, this battle of extremes did more harm than good, yielding little long-term benefit for the majority of Southern Baptists in the Middle.

Long before I transitioned into politics, I had already witnessed the politics of religion—especially in my denomination—playing out at the local and state levels. There were multiple inflexible litmus tests that one had to adhere to, starting with the understanding that no one could question the pastors and professors who had won the Battle for the Bible and the Southern Baptist Convention.

Over time, I came to understand that fear and self-protection were at the core of this division. I realized the church leadership's need to defend what they thought was right and what they thought was under attack. What I came to realize later in my pastoral career, however, was that much of what occurred during the Battle for the Bible wasn't truly about Christians discussing matters that deserved legitimate debate. Rather, it was a matter of *these* Christians arguing with *those* Christians about who was "right."

These were early, formative times in my career. After years of meeting people on both sides of these battles, I became even more convinced of the importance of seeking to understand before demanding to be understood.

When I graduated from the Southern Baptist Theological Seminary, one of my professors—who I greatly enjoyed and who had a front-row seat to the Southern Baptist battles—told me, "Whatever you do, don't bring the politics you learned into your pulpit."

Though I thought the professor's comment somewhat strange, given his experience and reputation, I accepted it as sage advice that there is a better way to work through our issues. I truly believe to this day that this mentor instilled in me a desire to find ways *through our division with people* rather than *through people with our divisions.*

When we founded Stonegate Fellowship Church in Midland in 1999, we started with about fifty families. By the time I stepped away from the pulpit in the fall of 2018, we had more than five thousand people attending services across multiple campuses. Even as a pastor, I witnessed extremes in the church. I'll admit, in my early days of preaching, I didn't always deliver the message of love and grace when it came to same-sex relationships. One Sunday, I told our congregation about the "perverted" relationship between actresses Ellen DeGeneres and Anne Heche, who were being referred to by the media as the "world's first gay super couple." As I described their relationship, I noticed many people in the pews nodding their heads in agreement.

The next day, however, a friend offered me wise counsel: "When you use words like *pervert* and *perversion*, people who are struggling, or just disagree with you, won't come talk to you because you've already labeled them." I was being challenged by the concept of how to disagree without disrespect; a relational reality that has now become even more of a conviction of mine in these days of the extremes. I apologized the following Sunday for leading the congregation down the wrong path. My convictions about relationships hadn't changed, but I recognized that my words and conduct had failed to show respect for our common humanity, and they did not leave the door open for honest conversation without disrespect. It was another turning point in our church to say, "We're not going to

Problem Solver

use our words to label, hurt, or disrespect people."

From that day forward, I vowed to follow the astute guidance of a counselor in Midland, who once told me, "I might not understand you or your issues, but I'll take a long walk with you toward Jesus, respect you, and we'll see what we discover."

Over the years, I had the privilege of walking alongside numerous individuals, couples, and families. The stories they shared often came from places of deep vulnerability and required tremendous trust. I had always tried to make it clear, both in my words and actions, that their stories mattered. My role was not to define people by their struggles but to walk with them through them.

Many of those conversations challenged my long-held beliefs and opinions. Still, I made a conscious choice not to shame or judge but rather to listen, to understand, and to find a way to share life together in mutual support. There were moments when we simply had to agree to disagree. But more often, we found ourselves on a journey together, doing what I've often described as "walking toward Jesus together."

But all of this was made possible because I valued our shared humanity even with our strong convictions. With this mindset we were able to walk through some difficult and often embarrassing stories. When the stories became public, we stood by our new friends, we had their back, and we wouldn't let others shame or ridicule them. Oftentimes, new chapters of hope and progress were written. Other times, the only solution was honor and love. But through it all, I tried my best to make sure we valued that person's life over his or her story.

The Middle

During my tenure as pastor, I walked with more than a few couples through times of crisis involving complicated and even life-threatening pregnancies. In a few cases, the doctors had advised them that the pregnancy would need to be terminated because the child's organs had not developed properly and the pregnancy would put the mother's life in danger. These were gut-wrenching, life-and-death situations and the worst kind of tragedy a couple could face. These matters did not neatly fit in the categories of the left and the right; they demanded listening, understanding, loving, and grieving together.

These experiences didn't change my views on abortion, but they dramatically altered my perception of people who were walking through these crises. I realized that these situations are sometimes not as cut-and-dried as I'd once assumed. Not every scared, expectant mother was either an "evil baby killer" or a "heroic baby saver." Rather, these were all fellow humans, going through difficult challenges, trying to navigate questions of life and death based on their beliefs of what is right and wrong.

The mother and father would sit across from me in tears, asking, "What do we do? We're going to be known as the people who had an abortion."

"You might be," I would tell them, "but I'm hearing your story." I would remind them that we were here to walk with them and seek to understand rather than demand to be understood. I reminded them we would walk with them through the struggle, no matter the choice they ultimately made. This did not compromise our convictions about right and wrong, but it forced us to listen to stories of real people facing real struggles—situations that rarely fit into the black-and-white thinking of the extremes.

People who attended our church or were even curious about us knew our statement of faith. But I did not want that statement of faith to get in the way of people who were searching for the Lord or going through struggles. One preacher said it well: "Just *belong* before you *believe*."

Of course, I wanted people to believe what we believed. Throughout my journey, I realized there might be times when we could not see eye to eye on matters of theology. However, we could find common ground in the fact that we are all humans created in the image of God, and we could still honor one another through our differences.

Our beliefs on matters of theology might endure, but respecting and honoring one another is a critical element of the Christian walk as well. This experience taught me that faith and its inherent conviction are about walking with people, regardless of whether they share your beliefs.

The extremes might say people must get their lives in order before they can belong to the church. The Middle says, "None of us are perfect, so let's walk together." Or, as Jesus said, "It is not the healthy who need a doctor, but the sick. I have not come to call the righteous, but sinners" (Mark 2:17 NIV).

This didn't mean there weren't real differences of opinion, fact, or even conviction, but there is a communal sense among the Middle that we are all still trying to figure life out, so let's lower the bar of perfection and raise the bar of our common humanity.

The Middle

My time at Stonegate Fellowship Church also introduced me to politics. Many of former President George W. Bush's childhood friends from Midland attended our church.

One of the president's friends carried a letter from me to President Bush at the White House, which led to a meeting I had with the president regarding human rights violations and religious freedom in China and Sudan. Through this experience, I realized the power of words and opportunity. I learned you must be ready to engage when given the chance because you never know what opportunities might come your way.

I once heard the claim, "You are five people removed from anyone in the world." This might sound impossible, but over the past twenty-five years, my own experiences have proved it to be true. But why does this matter in a book about the Middle? It matters because, later in this book, we will discuss our shared humanity and what we can each do to move away from the extremes.

You might think you cannot make an actual difference because you don't have an audience or an extended group of powerful friends. But the truth is, you never know whom your words and actions will influence—the world is truly a very small place. Those in the Middle—the majority of America—cannot underplay the hand of influence they have, whether at the dining room table, at PTA meetings, or even on people they don't know who might be influenced by their words and actions.

In 2019, just after I'd stepped down as pastor of Stonegate Fellowship Church, I was approached about running for mayor of Midland, one of the wealthiest and most conservative cities in the United States. According to the Bureau of Economic Analysis, Midland's per capita personal income was $143,469 in 2023, ranking it second among US metropolitan areas, behind only San Jose-Sunnyvale-Santa Clara, California, which had $148,036.[12] The reason Midland has such a wealthy population is that it is in the heart of the Permian Basin, one of the most prolific oil and natural gas regions in the world. The Permian Basin, which is found in western Texas and southeastern New Mexico, produces roughly 40 percent of US crude oil production. As of June 2024, the region's oil output reached about 6.3 million barrels per day.[13] Natural gas production was about 25.4 billion cubic feet per day.[14]

Midland has been regarded as a Republican stronghold for decades, and politicians at the state and national levels travel there every election to raise money. In recent presidential elections, Republican candidates received more than 70 to 80 percent of the vote in Midland. Former President George H. W. Bush moved to Midland with his wife, Barbara, and their son, George W. Bush, in 1948 to work in the oil industry. The family later moved to Houston, where George H. W. Bush became involved in politics. George W. Bush's childhood home in Midland is now a museum, commemorating the family's time in the city.

Running for mayor of Midland was not an easy decision for several reasons. First, I had simply not given it much thought and had no prior ambition for the office. Second, I had launched a consulting company that required focus, effort, travel, and time, so I wasn't sure I had the time to be mayor, if I even won. The only two compelling reasons for running for office were the number of people asking me to run—and a nagging sense that this unexpected opportunity might be a divine push to get in the political game.

One evening, I sat at the kitchen table and wrote out seven reasons why I shouldn't run. How could one argue with the perfect number seven? I walked over to my wife, handed her the list, and said, "Here you go. What do you think?"

She didn't even look at it. She handed the list back to me and said, "You know what you're supposed to do. You might as well admit it and get busy campaigning." That was it—from that moment we were in the race, and there was no turning back.

People experienced in local politics told me we'd know if we could win based on our ability to raise campaign funds. To my surprise, we not only raised funds but set a record for Midland mayoral contributions. Money was pouring in, our team was growing and strong, and our platform for doing everything we could to make Midland a top one hundred city in the country came together and gathered steam.

Despite having no platform and little prior interest in public office, I defeated a two-term incumbent. The next February, less than three months into my term, I faced one of the greatest challenges of my life. Everything we had planned and hoped for came to a screeching stop as COVID-19 shut down the world.

The reason I ran for office finally became clear to me: I had been called to shepherd a city through historical challenges. This wasn't my conclusion; it was the overwhelming sentiment of emails, texts, and conversations among voters as they sought to encourage my family and me in those most challenging, polarizing, and extreme days.

That wasn't the only realization I had during my early days in office. Now firmly in the public square and removed from the clergy class, I began to see and hear another perspective about how people in the church felt about the extremes behind sanctuary walls. Time after time, I met people in my office who had a church background but felt like they no longer had a home in the church. In most cases, they had made a mistake in the past, and someone from the conservative extreme had used it to convince them they were now an outsider, no longer welcome.

What was most alarming to me was how church leaders had used their mistakes to label people as *righteous* and *not so righteous*. Instead of using those experiences to help people become the best versions of themselves, they were held over their heads to make them feel less than others. These stories of real-life pain, induced by the extremes, were behind the reasons for seeking to make Stonegate Fellowship a place of second, third, and fourth chances. From outside the church and inside the public square, I was again reminded that the extremes are pushing us apart—and the Middle is being isolated, searching for fellowship, purpose, and understanding.

Some people may read this and be tempted to say that I must not have stood for anything. But every time I was confronted by those demanding perfection, I assumed two things: first, the perfection demanders (righteous extremists) often had issues they didn't want anyone to know about; and second, they had forgotten what

Jesus told the Pharisees when they brought a woman who had committed adultery: "Let him who is without sin among you be the first to throw a stone at her" (John 8:7).

Jesus challenged the religious extremists to examine their own sinfulness, and one by one, they left him in silence. Even today in America, it's easy to cast the first stone, so long as we avoid looking in the mirror while doing it.

As you can see, I've spent most of my life in the pew, the pulpit, and in politics. I came from a broken family and witnessed my mother, who was a divorcee, sit in the back of the church auditorium. During the Moral Majority 1980s, I watched as people who didn't agree with the churchgoing folks were considered evil or wicked, and it was up to the church to save them—or let them remain evil. Over time, I've realized that the enemy is the Enemy, not other people. I finally understood that one of our greatest mistakes is making enemies out of people rather than focusing on issues we can tackle together.

CHAPTER 3

Never Read the Comments

During my time as both a church pastor and later as the mayor of Midland, Texas, I often shared a simple but valuable piece of advice during sermons and city meetings: "Never read the comments."

Don't get me wrong—this wasn't an arrogant dismissal of public opinion or the beliefs of my congregation. It was a warning about the toxicity and distortion that can come from engaging with anonymous criticism or social media echo chambers. If you've ever ventured into the "For you" column on X or climbed down a rabbit hole on Facebook, you probably know exactly what I'm talking about.

Inevitably, someone would challenge me: "But how do you know what people are thinking and what matters to them?"

My answer was always the same: "I talk to them."

The Middle

On social media, opinions are often amplified by anger, sensationalism, clickbait, and controversy. As a pastor and mayor, I believed it was my duty as a leader to have authentic, face-to-face conversations with people sitting in the pews and those citizens who did or didn't vote for me. When I talked with residents over a cup of coffee or a beer, they were real conversations. There was room for empathy, context, and hopefully mutual understanding—even when we disagreed.

There's no doubt in my mind the proliferation of social media has exacerbated an "us versus them" mentality in America. Unfortunately, many of us don't understand that an algorithm feeds us stories we want to read and opinions we want to hear on social media. It's designed to keep us clicking and spending as much time as possible in front of a screen.

One of my greatest fears is that if we continue to allow algorithms to shape our opinions about important issues, we're going to inflict serious damage on our republic and on our people. Americans are going to have to get off social media and have meaningful conversations with other people to understand the full story of the world around them. Much of what we read and hear on social media—and even from mainstream news—is at best about 20 percent of the story. The information we consume in today's digital world is little more than sound bites and snippets of what's really happening around us, and more times than not, it lacks proper context—and sometimes, it's outright misinformation.

According to a 2020 study conducted by economists at Brown University, the United States has become politically polarized at a higher rate than any other major democracy in the world. The research found that affective polarization—"the extent to which citizens feel more negatively toward other political parties than toward their own"—more than doubled in the United States from 27.4 points in 1978 to 56.3 points in 2020.[15]

The study noted that affective polarization declined in Japan, Australia, Norway, Sweden, and Germany, and rose only slightly in Switzerland, France, Canada, and New Zealand during the same time period.[16]

It is becoming increasingly clear that the staggering political polarization in the United States, in part, can be attributed to the rise of the Internet and social media over the past decade. If you haven't watched the Netflix documentary *The Social Dilemma*, I highly recommend it. Some of the same Big Tech experts who created the social networking used by Facebook, X, and Instagram pull back the curtain on how these companies employ algorithms to manipulate and influence users.

In the film, Edward Tufte, professor emeritus of computer science, political science, and statistics at Yale University, said, "There are only two industries that call their customers 'users': illegal drugs and software."[17] Indeed, social media companies are aware that when their users receive "likes" and scroll through content for hours, they get a dopamine hit in their brains much like when gambling or using drugs.

Unfortunately, negative side effects of these algorithms include creating informational echo chambers, spreading false information, and introducing users to communities with extreme, potentially harmful ideologies. Over the past decade, these factors have contributed to increasing distrust of media and government, contributed to growth in domestic terrorism, and increased political polarization across the United States.

Our extremism has been exacerbated by the noise of social media. We have truly lost our minds if we believe the unhinged battleground of social media is the way to unite and move forward as a nation. The Middle has grown tired of keyboard warriors and talking-point pundits. Though it sounds old-fashioned—and is more difficult now than ever—it's time to sit knee-to-knee and eyeball-to-eyeball, talk through our issues, and find a better way for all of us.

There was a time, even in the not so distant past, when Democrats and Republicans found ways to get together and work toward common ground. Decades ago, when I spoke to a group of seasoned politicians and lobbyists in Washington, DC, a longtime political journalist told me, "I can remember living in this city when Republicans and Democrats finished their days having a drink with each other, discussing issues, and trying to come up with policies to get to the answer. Those days are over."

While it is difficult to accurately pinpoint when the United States took such a dramatic turn toward an "us versus them" battleground—particularly for politicians and others seeking power and influence—it's probably safe to assume that divisive rhetoric has been a part of American life since the country's founding.

One might argue it has been part of humanity since the garden of Eden when Adam blamed Eve and Eve blamed the serpent. It seems to be wired into our human nature to accuse the other person of wrongdoing before we take a hard look at how *we* might be part of the problem—if not the *entire* problem.

It's probably no coincidence that when the Founding Fathers drafted the original document for our first system of government at the Constitutional Convention in 1787, they didn't mention political parties. In fact, George Washington, John Adams, Benjamin Franklin, and others probably wanted to avoid the political divisions that had caused many of their ancestors to flee England during the bloody civil wars of the seventeenth century.

Consider what the Founding Fathers wrote or said about political parties and the threat of extremism more than two centuries ago: Alexander Hamilton, the first secretary of the treasury, called political parties "the most fatal disease" of popular governments and hoped his new country would avoid them.[18] James Madison, the "Father of the Constitution," wrote in "Federalist No. 10" that among the "advantages promised by a well-constructed Union, none deserves to be more accurately developed than its tendency to break and control the violence of faction."[19]

During debates in Philadelphia that summer, Hamilton and Madison noted that the Constitution's "spirit of moderation" contrasted with the "intolerant spirit" of those who are "ever so much persuaded of their being in the right in any controversy."[20]

Adams, the first US vice president and second president, said, "Without the great political virtues of humility, patience, and moderation . . . every man in power becomes a ravenous beast of prey."[21] Jefferson, the primary author of the Declaration of Independence, wrote years later, "Men by their constitutions are naturally divided into two parties."[22]

Washington, the first and only independent president in US history, warned of political extremism and factions as he took office—and again eight years later when he announced he wouldn't seek a third term. Washington, an avid reader of the early eighteenth-century English essayist Joseph Addison, found prophetic words in Addison's "The Malice of Parties" letter, which stated,

> There cannot a greater judgment befall a country than a dreadful spirit of division as rends a government into two distinct people, and makes them greater strangers, and more averse to one another, than if they were actually two different nations. . . . This influence is very fatal both to men's morals and their understandings; it sinks the virtue of a nation, and not only so, but destroys even common sense.[23]

Washington witnessed differing political views tear apart his cabinet. Hamilton desired a strong central government, while Madison and Jefferson opposed a national banking system and championed free markets and trade. Hamilton's conservative Federalist Party dominated the national government beginning in 1789. In response, Jefferson and Madison founded the Democratic-Republican (the forerunner to the modern Democratic Party) three years later.

In Washington's farewell address on September 17, 1796, he

warned Americans of the "baneful effects of the Spirit of Party."

"Generally this spirit, unfortunately, is inseparable from our nature, having roots in the strongest passions of the human mind," Washington wrote. "It exists under different stages in all governments, more or less stifled, controlled, or repressed; but, in those of the popular form it is seen in its greatest rankness and is truly their worst enemy."[24]

In his 2012 book *The 3rd Alternative*, author and educator Stephen R. Covey warned Americans of the coming social wars:

> The twentieth century was an age of impersonal war, but the twenty-first seems like an age of personal malice. The rage thermometer is way up. Families quarrel, co-workers contend, cyber bullies terrorize, courts are jammed, and fanatics murder the innocent. Contemptuous "commentators" swamp the media—the more outrageous their attacks, the more money they make. The rising fever of contention can make us ill.[25]

In a December 2010 TED Talk titled "Take the Other to Lunch," wellness expert Elizabeth Lesser voiced concerns about "negative otherizing," which dehumanizes individuals and perpetuates stereotypes. She mentioned popular political books of the time, including *Liberalism Is a Mental Disorder*, *Arguing with Idiots*, *Pinheads and Patriots*, and *Rush Limbaugh Is a Big, Fat Idiot*.

"I'm deeply disturbed by the ways in which all of our cultures are demonizing the other, by the voice we're giving to the most decisive among us," Lesser said in the TED Talk. "The worst eras in human history start like this, with negative otherizing, and then they morph into violent extremism."[26] Lesser argued that "negative otherizing" is how genocides started in Europe at the hands of the Nazis, in Cambodia by the Khmer Rouge under Pol Pot, and in Rwanda, where some eight hundred thousand members of the Tutsi ethnic group were slaughtered by ethnic Hutu extremists.

Of course, it's important to note that Lesser's comments and Covey's words came more than a decade ago, before social media fully exploded in the United States and algorithms took control of what we see and thereby what we often conclude about others.

Sadly, we have fully immersed ourselves in shaping our impressions of others through snapshots, reels, and headlines that lack context and/or accuracy. We no longer have a shared humanity and have succumbed to Lesser's "otherizing," in which each day is a battle between "us" and "them."

One might even suggest that "otherizing" has given way to "objectifying" in America, wherein those of differing opinions are viewed only as objects of rage or approval without a proper understanding of the other person or an appreciation of their humanity. Worst of all, this "otherizing" cuts both ways; this is not a one-sided problem for either Democrats or Republicans.

Political extremism in the United States is nothing new, but it has intensified dramatically during the social media era. The religious awakening led by the Christian right and Jerry Falwell's Moral Majority, in response to the social and cultural transformations of the sixties and seventies, intensified differences between the political parties. Over the past fifty years, these differences have been exacerbated, leaving America in its current state of "us versus them."

My own evangelical experience did not escape this trend of "otherizing" or "objectifying" of the other side. I witnessed assumptions being made about people who lived a different lifestyle or simply asked questions that made the established orthodoxy a bit nervous. People who said *those things*, drank alcohol, or listened or danced to that type of music were categorized, "otherized," or simply viewed as someone in desperate need of conversion.

However, the people on the other side were rarely viewed as fellow human beings deserving of respect. Instead, their behaviors were criticized by those who were most adept at sin management and behavior modification—none of whom could actually throw the first stone if it came down to it.

This attitude of "us versus them" cut from right to left in theological circles, regardless of whether either side wanted to admit it or not. We objectified and "otherized," and along the way, we forgot that everyone shares an equal Creator and has inherent value—if we truly believe the Bible both sides claimed to read.

In a strictly theocratic view, the notion of a righteous divide was seen as absolute truth. However, another theological perspective calls to mind Jesus's New Testament command to "Love your enemies and pray for those who persecute you" (Matthew 5:44 NIV). Despite this, the prevailing "us versus them" rhetoric became a rallying cry, deepening divisions. Republicans increasingly aligned themselves with the religious right, while the left was often labeled as godless.

Over time, no issue seemed to fuel this divide more than the

The Middle

Supreme Court's 1973 *Roe v. Wade* decision. There are certainly serious moral arguments to be made about this issue, but it seemed that when "otherizing" occurred, productive and well-intentioned discussion ceased. Now, decades later, even after *Roe v. Wade* was overturned by the Supreme Court, abortion rates haven't slowed. Instead, a growing number of people are seeking abortions through different means, such as the abortion pill. The sides keep fighting over the issue, but they've yet to sit down together as fellow humans and find a way to discuss even the most divisive issues.

The relentless rhetoric between the left and right rarely subsides, except during national emergencies such as natural disasters, terrorist attacks, or wars. In those moments, we see the very qualities of humanity that those in the Middle aspire to uphold all the time. Those moments prove that when leadership or circumstances provide a significant cause, our common humanity will rise to the top. However, in the absence of this common vision, we tend to revert to the extremes of individualism.

On April 19, 1995, I exited my car only five miles from the Alfred P. Murrah Federal Building in Oklahoma City. I heard an enormous explosion and assumed there had been an ordinance mishap in the nearby Air Force base. This was before the Internet and cell phones had become popular, so immediate information was scarce. We could only wait in our offices, watching TV news reports and helicopter footage of the tragic events. In the end, the deadliest domestic terrorist attack in US history claimed 168 lives—including 19 children—and injured more than 600 others.

In mere moments, the entire Oklahoma City community

rallied to support the families of those lost and the survivors left injured. Not since the tragic assassinations of the 1960s—when John F. Kennedy, Martin Luther King Jr., and Robert F. Kennedy were taken from us—had our nation come together with such unity, dissolving the divide between the far right and far left.

Six years later, America came together again after the terrorist attacks of September 11, 2001. Those attacks, carried out by nineteen hijackers affiliated with the militant Islamist extremist group Al-Qaeda, senselessly snuffed out 2,977 lives when airliners crashed into the World Trade Center in New York; the Pentagon in Arlington, Virginia; and a field in Shanksville, Pennsylvania. It was the deadliest terrorist act in world history and the most stunning day we'd ever experienced in America.

In the days, weeks, and months following the September 11 attacks, we didn't identify ourselves as Democrats or Republicans, conservatives or liberals. For a brief moment, at least, as our country picked itself up off the mat and went after the terrorists behind the attacks, we were simply Americans.

The two-party system in America, by all indications, seems to have originated in the presidential election of 1796 between Adams and Jefferson. But it wasn't the birth of a two-party system that has led us to the precarious position where we are today, with the left and right tearing us apart at the middle.

There are always two sides to a debate, if not three or four. The two-party system, though decried by Washington, has existed for more than two centuries. But a twenty-first-century world might finally be waking up to the idea that commitment to party is not the indication of commitment to country. Instead, the two-party system has done more to divide allegiance to the American ideal and dream. The Middle is sensing a wake-up call—to allegiance to this ideal and dream rather than the control and manipulation of the party apparatus and platform.

Indeed, we were a nation divided by extremes leading up to the American Civil War. This should be a warning to us of what happens when extreme views take hold and there is an unwillingness to find the better path—the third way.

As I'll argue throughout this book, the Civil War was rooted in the very issues we face today: a lack of honor and respect for our common humanity and an unwillingness to stand united as Americans. The deep divide between the North and the South in the 1860s serves as a case study on what happens when we "otherize" or objectify those with whom we disagree. When the conversation ceases and the caricatures take hold, the die is cast, the paradigm is sealed, and the extremes become entrenched.

The result, as history has proven, is war.

CHAPTER 4

An Unmitigated Mess

As President Abraham Lincoln was leading the country through its nadir, the dreadful Civil War of the 1860s, one of his closest friends and allies warned him, "The time is coming when we shall have to all be either Abolitionists or Democrats."[27]

As America was on the verge of a bloody four-year conflict that would ultimately kill an estimated 620,000 men—about 2 percent of the country's population at the time—Lincoln left the collapsing Whig Party for the newly formed Republican Party, which opposed slavery expansion. In so many words, Lincoln's ally told Lincoln that the country's middle was eroding, and its people would soon have to align with either the Abolitionist cause or the Democratic Party, which at the time was mostly pro-slavery.

Even more than one hundred and fifty years ago, there were

two loud extremes in America—and an increasingly shrinking middle ground.

Before Lincoln had been elected America's sixteenth president in 1860, he warned its citizens of the oncoming crisis over slavery. During Lincoln's famous "House Divided" speech at the Illinois Republican State Convention in Springfield on June 16, 1858, he forewarned of the dire consequences of the brewing deep division that would one day lead to the American Civil War.

Utilizing biblical imagery from Mark 3:25, Lincoln argued,

> A house divided against itself cannot stand, I believe this government cannot endure, permanently half slave and half free. I do not expect the Union to be dissolved—I do not expect the house to fall—but I do expect it will cease to be divided. It will become all one thing, or all the other.
>
> Either the opponents of slavery, will arrest the further spread of it, and place it where the public mind shall rest in the belief that it is in course of ultimate extinction; or its advocates will push it forward till it shall become alike lawful in all the States, old as well as new—North as well as South.[28]

Clearly, this isn't the first time our country has been divided over discordant issues. While Lincoln might be revered as one of America's greatest leaders, even the radical extremists who became increasingly powerful during the deepening polarization of the time reviled him. In her 2005 book, *Team of Rivals: The Political Genius of Abraham Lincoln*, historian Doris Kearns Goodwin noted, "The center was being drained while both extremes were hunkering down with rampant animosity."[29]

While the America of today is thankfully not on the verge of another Civil War, our political divisions seem just as deep as ever—and continue to widen. While Americans aren't taking up arms on blood-soaked battlefields to defend their political views, we are battling one another with verbal weapons in Facebook messages and 280-character posts on X.

When assessing the current crisis in our country, it's probably easiest to point to the 2024 US presidential election. A national poll conducted found that only 40 percent of Americans had a favorable view of then-President Joe Biden, while 55 percent had an unfavorable one.[30] The numbers were nearly as bad for his Republican challenger—and eventual winner—former President Donald Trump, who registered 43 percent favorable and 53 percent unfavorable.[31]

If Biden hadn't dropped out of his reelection campaign and endorsed his vice president, Kamala Harris, the presidential election of 2024 would have been one of the most unpopular matchups in US history. Only during the 2016 presidential election, when Trump defeated Hillary Clinton, did Americans think less of both candidates.[32]

In fact, there was so much dislike for Biden, Harris, and Trump in the months leading up to the 2024 presidential election that analysts recycled a political term from eight years earlier, "double haters," to describe Americans who probably wouldn't have voted for either candidate.

Remarkably, Americans are even more disillusioned about the job that Congress is doing on Capitol Hill. A 2024 Gallup poll found that 81 percent of Americans disapproved of the way Congress is handling its job, while only 13 percent approved.[33]

For many voters, the 2024 presidential campaign and election was one of contrasting visions of extreme reaction rather than a presidential preference. While some Americans might disagree, even though Trump ultimately won the popular vote and the Electoral College, Republicans maintained the Senate and House of Representatives with the slimmest of margins—flipping four seats in the Senate to control a 53–47 majority and nine seats in the House to hold a 220–215 edge. This reveals the truth that most of the country's voting public remains firmly in the center when choosing whom to trust with shaping national policy.

While some might argue the president makes policy, this is another area in which we are an unmitigated mess. Over the past two decades, every presidential transition has resulted in the mass issuing of executive orders. On average, the ten presidents before Trump's second term each issued about 266 orders during their time in office.[34] Of course, many of those executive orders are quickly rescinded, and Congress ultimately does nothing to act on them over the ensuing four years. This is not what the Founding Fathers intended with the separation of powers.

Rather than tackling crime, immigration, health care, or other important issues of national concern, Congress sits in gridlock and passes continuing resolutions to prevent government shutdowns, while those citizens in the Middle are left in limbo, wondering what the elected politicians they sent to Washington, DC, are even doing.

Every four years, almost like clockwork, campaign rhetoric is met with inaction once an election ends. Promises of new infrastructure, lower taxes, expanded health care, the rich paying their fair share, and other campaign platforms turn out to be hollow. The list goes on and returns in different slogans every two to four years, but little changes. Make no mistake: Our proverbial house is in chaos, yet we persist in vilifying one another, stalling any meaningful progress.

More than ever, we need leaders like Lincoln, who reunited the country after the Civil War and ended the country's dehumanizing system of slavery. We need the resolve of Franklin D. Roosevelt, who took office during the worst of the Great Depression, but assured Americans, "The only thing we have to fear is fear itself."[35] FDR also led the United States through the frightening times of World War II. And though Lyndon B. Johnson had his faults when it came to the Vietnam War, he assumed the presidency at one of the country's low points, after the assassination of John F. Kennedy on November 22, 1963, and helped the country bounce back by enacting the landmark Civil Rights Act. Most of all, LBJ urged Americans to "build a Great Society, a place where the meaning of man's life matches the marvels of man's labor."[36]

Adding to the current toxic mixture in America today is even more voter cynicism about the mainstream media. An October 2024 poll by Gallup found that only 8 percent of Americans have a "great deal" of trust and confidence in the media to report "fully, accurately, and fairly," while only 23 percent said they had a "fair amount" of trust.[37] Strikingly, 36 percent of the respondents said they had no confidence at all in the media.

According to Gallup's poll on the media the prior year, it was the first time since 1974 that the percentage of Americans with no trust at all in the media was higher than the combined percentage with a great deal or fair amount of trust.

Even as this book is being written, there are exposés regarding the media's cover-up of President Joe Biden's mental struggles in his final days of office. The American people saw this decline in Biden's infamous debate performance with then-candidate Donald Trump and had to wonder why there was such a difference in perception by the left and the right.

While the Middle interpreted Joe Biden's appearance with common sense, the extremes battled it out in such a way that led to media mea culpas after Trump came into office. The Middle was not buying into either side's caricatures of the candidates but instead was interpreting what they were seeing and hearing through common sense and decency—attributes the extremes seem to avoid while the Middle continues to wonder where these qualities of our common humanity went. Where have you gone Walter Cronkite, Peter Jennings, and Edward R. Murrow?

Living in today's digital world, Americans have dramatically altered the way they consume news. A Pew Research Center survey in September 2024 found that an overwhelming number of adults in the United States (54 percent) get news from a smartphone, computer, or tablet at least some of the time, including 25 percent who say they do so often.[38]

Another Pew Research Center survey in May 2024 found that 32 percent of the respondents said they prefer to get news from TV at least sometimes. The data for print news and radio outlets is even more alarming: Only 26 percent of US adults reported getting local news from news websites and only 9 percent from print newspapers and radio stations—the lowest numbers ever recorded by the Pew Research Center.[39]

In a fragmented world with so many online news outlets, Americans are consuming "nightly news" moment by moment in thirty-second clips of information that are being filtered by whoever is posting them and are being delivered to consumers on social media by the algorithms we talked about in the last chapter. Depending on the news outlets, they continue to amplify the extremes on both sides.

As a result, Americans' distrust of the so-called establishment of government and media has left many seeking whatever narrative they can find to suit their predetermined views. This trifecta of terror poses a significant threat to the future of our country. Americans want to trust the people they send to Washington, DC. People in the Middle are simply trying to live their lives—caring for their families and jobs, looking out for their neighbors and communities, and participating in local events. They're not typically concerned with what happens in city hall, the state legislature, or Congress. However, as America has grown and life has changed dramatically, the federal government has taken on a larger and more influential role in daily life. With the national debt nearing 100 percent of GDP, it's clear that the federal government has expanded while Main Street has shrunk. This didn't happen overnight. Over the past few decades, Americans have voted for politicians who promised to rein in government spending, only to realize that these politicians favored K Street over Main Street.

Much of the dysfunction in Washington, DC, comes from a powerful idea that has grown over the decades: That the government is here to serve and meet its citizens' needs. This idea can be traced back to FDR's New Deal, which aimed to provide relief, recovery, and reform through federal intervention in the economy following the Great Depression. It could similarly be tied to LBJ's Great Society, which focused on the War on Poverty, civil rights, health care, and education. Through those federal relief programs and the ensuing ones like them, the power of government—and the widely accepted narrative that the government knows best—led to a form of government the Founding Fathers never intended. One of the overriding narratives in our country's birth was the call to self-governance. Early Americans wanted to live their lives and pursue their dreams without a government telling them what to do, taxing them too much, or encouraging them what to believe.

There was a basic axiom that, together, Americans could solve their problems at a local level. Of course, over time, advances in communication, national defense, and transportation demanded a collective federal effort to make things work. But eventually, these necessary federal efforts opened the door to increasing infringement around the kitchen table.

An Unmitigated Mess

Money remains the lifeblood of politics, and nothing has affected the extremes more than the mighty dollar. In the 2024 election, candidates, their political parties, super PACs, and other outside groups spent nearly $16 billion on the presidential and congressional elections, according to the election transparency nonprofit OpenSecrets. Much of that money was spent on TV campaign ads in battleground states like Pennsylvania ($65 million), Michigan ($36 million), and Georgia ($33 million).[40]

The amount of money being dumped into politics, and the control that comes with it, makes 1 Timothy 6:10 ring true: "The love of money is a root of all kinds of evils." While the Bible warns us of greed and the destructive consequences of valuing wealth over faith and righteousness, money pays for attention and action from the extremes of local, state, and national politics, and from K Street to Wall Street, coast to coast.

Worst of all, given the current political climate, you must talk and act in extremes to even be elected in America. David W. Brady, a professor emeritus of political economy at Stanford University and a senior fellow at the Hoover Institution, argued that one of the biggest reasons Congress is dysfunctional is because there are no longer conservative Democrats or liberal Republicans, like there were in the seventies and eighties. Brady stated:

> It was harder for Democrats to bad-mouth conservatives. It was harder for Republicans to totally bad-mouth liberals because they had some in their own party and needed them. So there was always that mitigating factor.

That's gone. Moderates don't run anymore. A Democrat or a Republican who's toward the middle, they get beat in primaries. So that pushes Democrats further left and Republicans further right and you can't get legislation. That increases polarization.[41]

A few years ago, when I helped a friend run for political office in Texas, we found ourselves working to not get outflanked by the far right.

My friend and I were both Republicans.

Author and entrepreneur David Dodson, another Stanford lecturer, ran for the US Senate in Wyoming as a Republican in 2018. Incumbent John Barrasso, who has held the seat since 2007, soundly defeated him. One of Dodson's biggest realizations during the election was that "polarization and partisanship are what both parties want because the one thing they can agree on is dividing the population into a red camp and a blue camp and then gerrymandering like crazy."[42]

"If you're running for a House district, you're going to get penalized for working with the other side," Dodson said. "If you want to get elected, you don't want to talk to the middle, because the middle is going to alienate you from the people who are going to show up to vote in the primary. You need to talk in extremes."[43]

Dodson contended that's the reason why so many Republican politicians argued that the Democrats stole the 2020 presidential election from Trump, even if it wasn't true. "That's what their customers want to hear," Dodson said.[44]

An Unmitigated Mess

With $26 million spent on every vote on K Street, Main Street's voice is heard only on Election Day. What matters to K Street holds more weight from the time a politician is sworn in until he or she leaves office. This cycle continues with their next terms or successors. In Washington, DC, and state capitals, new legislators are often reminded by their parties to align with their platforms to receive reelection support, regardless of what they might have promised voters during their campaigns. As a result, nothing gets done in government, and those in the Middle view the situation with sharp suspicion.

As the former mayor of Midland, Texas, I still remember when I was first confronted with this power reality as it pertains to state and federal politics. Shortly after I took office, a state politician told me, "It doesn't matter what you say on the campaign trail. When you get to the capital, the party powers will make sure you toe the line—or you won't get a good committee seat."

While serving as mayor, I once told our city attorney, "You know, I don't get any calls from people asking me to vote a certain way or do something for them." His reply was short and to the point: "It's because they know you think for yourself."

When the extremes control the levers of power at the local, state, and national levels, Main Street has no alternative but to be cynical toward the entire process, which seems to forget about them as soon as an election is over.

Of course, when the same politicians are reelected year after year without making progress, apathy sets in on Main Street, which is the most difficult pill to swallow. While those in the Middle want to be left alone by the government, the radical left and right seize control and push through legislation to meet their own agendas. Even if the elected politicians aren't representing them, people in the Middle tend to say, "It is what it is" out of frustration.

This unmitigated mess of media, money, and dysfunction is symptomatic of a country that has lost its moral center and high ground. The Founding Fathers made much of the idea that only moral people of great inner character are capable of self-governance.

As Benjamin Franklin and other delegates were leaving Independence Hall in Philadelphia at the Constitutional Convention in 1787, a woman reportedly asked him, "Well, Doctor, what have we got, a republic or a monarchy?"

Franklin famously answered, "A republic, if you can keep it."[45]

More than anything else, a republic requires a citizenry with respect for one another and a willingness to work together rather than against one another. Jesus said, "You shall love your neighbor as yourself" (Matthew 22:39 NKJV). Perhaps our moral center needs to be reestablished by each one of us learning how to get comfortable with what's inside of us and who we are before we start engaging people only by what we see and hear from them.

Over the years, I have grown fond of a phrase I have found to be true: "Hurt people hurt people." As difficult as it might be, we must come to grips with the unmitigated mess inside of us before we can begin productive work together through the unmitigated messes all around us.

CHAPTER 5

Tribal Instincts

Long before European settlers discovered what would become America, five Native tribes in what are now upstate New York, northern Pennsylvania, and parts of Ontario and Quebec were engaged in constant fighting and raiding. The Mohawk, Oneida, Onondaga, Cayuga, and Seneca tribes fought so much among themselves that they were on the verge of extinguishing one another, even before colonists introduced disease and more bloodshed during the conquests of their lands.

Sometime between 1450 and 1600, according to Native American lore, a great prophet sent by the Creator traveled those lands, spreading his message of peace among the warring tribes. His name was Dekanawidah, or the Great Peacemaker, and he claimed to be the son of a virgin mother. Along with the spiritual leader Hiawatha, Dekanawidah urged the five tribes to form a nation-state that would rule with wisdom rather than conflict.

The legend goes that Dekanawidah told tribal leaders that he would plant a Great Tree of Peace. Its branches would protect the people, and its "white roots of truth" would stretch north, east, south, and west, spreading news of peace to all tribes.[46] Dekanawidah instructed warriors to bury their weapons, and he planted the Great Tree of Peace on top of them.

To ensure that every voice was heard during the ensuing peace negotiations, Dekanawidah introduced a talking stick to identify the speaker during the council. No one was allowed to interrupt until the person speaking passed the talking stick to someone else. According to legend, the talking stick gave a speaker the power to tell the truth and speak from the heart. Among many tribes, the person taking possession of the talking stick waited a few minutes to talk, ensuring that he didn't speak hastily and didn't say something he would later regret.

After long negotiations, the five feuding tribes reached a peace accord, forming the Iroquois Confederacy, which later became the Six Nations when the Tuscarora joined the confederacy in 1722. The nations were bound by a central constitution and a common set of laws, and their common council consisted of clan and village chiefs. Each tribe had one vote, and decisions were passed only with a unanimous vote. The Six Nations' early democracy became an inspiration for the thirteen colonies of the United States.

If you've watched the endless shouting between political pundits and politicians across the media and news landscape, you are more than aware that America could use a talking stick today.

Our political history and landscape resemble a kaleidoscope of near-religious fervor. Because of the proliferation of the Internet, author Seth W. Godin argued in his book *Tribes: We Need You to Lead Us* that there are more tribes in America than ever before:

> Existing tribes are bigger, but more important, it means that there are now more tribes, smaller tribes, influential tribes, horizontal and vertical tribes, and tribes that could never have existed before. Tribes you work with, tribes you travel with, tribes you buy with. Tribes that vote, that discuss, that fight. Tribes where everyone knows your name.[47]

Think about your friends and the people you surround yourself with. We have tribes at our golf clubs. Tribes at school. Tribes at work. Tribes that follow their favorite college football or pro sports teams. Blue-collar and white-collar tribes. Military veteran tribes. First responder tribes. Religious tribes. Country music tribes. Grateful Dead tribes. And, yes, political tribes.

Our tribes establish rules of conduct and belief, and tribal chieftains who serve as spokespersons and authorities lead them. Our tribes—social and political—have rituals of membership, dress, behavior, and even actions toward those who seemingly break with the tribe. Our tribes look down on those who might have different rituals than ours, speak in other languages, or even disagree with us. If you don't look, act, and talk like our tribe, then you are considered a threat.

Once these tribes are established, as Godin pointed out, the only name for those who challenge their rituals and established beliefs is *heretic*. They're the troublemakers or rebels rocking the boat, whether it's in business, politics, religion, or culture. However, Godin argued that the leader of every major movement, innovation, or revolution was someone who had the courage to defy tradition and a tribe's established mentality, inspiring a new way of thinking.

"Heretics are the new leaders," Godin wrote. "The ones who challenge the status quo, who get out in front of their tribes, who create movements."[48]

Being a heretic in America's political landscape isn't easy. To challenge the accepted religion of the left and right political tribes is to threaten the faith people have invested in these narrow tribes. Conversely, the faith of the Middle is rooted in the confession that all men are created equal and are endowed by their Creator with certain inalienable rights: life, liberty, and the pursuit of happiness. The faith of the Middle is rooted in the integrity, character, and actions of those who truly stand in the majority middle rather than in the boisterous claims of the extremes.

The heretic of the Middle may not at first be welcomed with open arms, but he or she will challenge the claims of the extremes to protect the pursuit and true faith of the American dream. The Middle believes that actions speak louder than words, and when disagreement leads to constant disrespect, the religious fervor of the tribe has overtaken the faithful pursuit of the larger objective of "One nation, under God."

There's no question we're more comfortable when we build our lives around people who are similar to us. We work, play, congregate, and generally like to have people around us and in our circles that demand the least amount of flexibility and change. This is not a good or bad thing; it's just the way it is. I remember the old saying my teachers used to repeat, "Birds of a feather flock together." However, this self-selecting isolationism often guards and protects us from the wider world of shared humanity to which we all belong, especially in the United States.

I am concerned that our ever-widening division into identity groups, political factions, and guardians of viewpoints and lifestyles has led to a state of affairs where we too easily forget our shared identity as human beings—cohabitators on a rock revolving around the sun. We are losing sight of who we are together because we have grown so far apart that we can no longer see the other side.

From the time God introduced Adam and Eve into the garden of Eden—or, depending on your beliefs, from the time cavemen learned to use their hands and discovered fire—living in tightly knit groups was crucial for survival. Cooperation was necessary in hunting and foraging for food in a world with limited resources and harsh conditions, and it was paramount in protecting tribe members from predators—and enemies—from outside the group. From the very beginning of time, humans lived in small groups, usually made up mostly of relatives and others with shared identities and values. Interactions with strangers were rare, and those seeking to join the tribe were met with skepticism—often viewed as a threat to the tribe's survival.

"We wouldn't have civilizations if we didn't create groups," said Lilliana Mason, a political scientist at Johns Hopkins University and author of *Uncivil Agreement: How Politics Became Our Identity*. "We are designed to form groups, and the only way to define a group is there has to be someone who's not in it."[49]

However, our political groupings—whether progressive, conservative, Libertarian, socialist, centrist, Democrat, Republican, or independent—have taken on the trappings of religion. Religious groupings have a strict set of rules that members must follow that are based on systems and structures developed over time to dictate and determine behaviors.

Don't get me wrong—I'm not talking about faith. Every person is a person of faith, even the atheist. Each of us is wired to place our faith and trust in that person or thing that offers us the best hope for our best life. But too often, the trappings of religion cheapen our faith in something or someone. Religion groups us with people who act, talk, and sometimes believe like we do, giving us a warm feeling that all is good and in order as long as we stay in the tribe of our religion. And, as Godin noted, anyone who calls into question the religion (the tribe) is labeled a heretic.

I belonged to a tribe called the Southern Baptist Convention (SBC) for most of my life. Though faith was a component of this tribe, it was primarily a religion. There was a creed—"The Baptist Faith and Message"—that was hotly debated and at times changed. It was often used as a litmus test of whether you were a "true" Southern Baptist. The SBC had a large headquarters and leaders who had risen to a lofty status, becoming qualified chieftains of the tribe. There were annual conventions where the tribe gathered and voted on matters of faith and conscience.

The leaders decided where the congregation would hang its collective hat of conviction and belief. We questioned whether members of other tribes were true believers, as their confessions, creeds, and rules were different from ours—and therefore must be wrong. And like in other tribes and religions, people were highly discouraged from questioning the creed, unless one wanted to be labeled a heretic.

I experienced this tribal power and found myself in the position of a heretic when I became a pastor of a local church. In my studies and meditations, I questioned the leadership structure taught by the tribe. There's no need to go into the minute details, except to say I questioned the authority and power structure that many had come to see as infallible.

Predictably, I became a heretic for looking outside the tribe—and even into other tribes—to find a better way. I had to accept that I was going to be ostracized by my own big, popular tribe and be forced to find another one—or, better yet, become a pioneer, content as a tribe of one.

The heretic occasionally gets an audience, and over time, the audience listens to the heretic and realizes he or she is not trying to *destroy faith* but simply *reform religion*. As the audience grows larger, curiosity spreads among other tribesmen (and women). They begin to see the greater quest of faith, which is the pursuit of trust and community. In the end, extreme tribes are recognized for what they have often become: groups seeking to control, often through perceived knowledge, authority, power, and even fear that you'll die if you leave the tribe.

I'm happy to report that the heretical questions I began to ask about structure eventually became a movement by others within the convention. What was once considered heresy has now become expanded practice, even within my old Southern Baptist tribe.

Our political extremes and their followers are like the religious tribes I've described. Across the spectrum of left and right, tribes of true believers gather under banners, podcasts, newscasts, and self-appointed leaders. These political tribes take on nearly mythical status and authority with creeds and confessions of what's right and wrong. They are populated by people of faith—faith in America and the Constitution, as they see it—who often lose sight of the journey of faith in the American dream. They guard, protect, and defend one another from those who question or call into doubt their creed (the heretics). After all, no "true American" would call into question the leaders of the tribes camped out on the left and the right.

Above all, the Middle is a call to the heretics. These heretics have great faith but have begun to see the tribes as people who are more interested in protecting than discovering. If you dare go outside the tribe, you'll face the wrath of those you left behind. The sad reality is that the people in the tribes in America aren't all that different. They've simply been told over and over by their leaders that people who look different, act differently, and believe differently are wrong—or even evil.

Consider the groundbreaking study conducted seventy years ago by social psychologist Muzafer Sherif and his colleagues at

Robber's Cave, an Oklahoma state park near one of the outlaw Jesse James's hideouts. During the summer of 1954, two groups of eleven- and twelve-year-old boys—white, Protestant, and middle-class—were brought to the park on separate buses. They were placed in different bunkhouses and were unaware of the other group's existence. Quickly, the boys formed friendships and shared identities; one group called itself the Rattlers, and the other, the Eagles.

The researchers hypothesized that when groups have conflicting aims—"when one can achieve its ends only at the expense of the other"—they become hostile.[50] It was an accurate assumption as the boys clashed in a series of baseball, football, treasure hunt, and tug-of-war competitions.

"The tournament started in a spirit of good sportsmanship," Sherif wrote. "But as it progressed, good feeling soon evaporated. The members of each group began to call their rivals 'stinkers,' 'sneaks,' and 'cheaters.' They refused to have anything to do with individuals in the opposing group."[51]

Hostilities escalated with one group burning the other's banner at a baseball field. The boys planned raids, hoarding green apples as ammunition, and scuffles and name-calling became the norm. The researchers observed that only when the groups faced a mutual crisis—busted water lines, insufficient money for a movie, and a broken-down food truck—did they begin to work together. In the end, they had a joint campfire, presented skits and sang songs together, and even traveled home on the same bus.

"What our limited experiments have shown is that the possibilities for achieving harmony are greatly enhanced when groups are brought together to work toward common ends," Sherif wrote. "Then favorable information about a disliked group is seen in a new light, and leaders are able to take bolder steps toward cooperation. In short, hostility gives way when groups pull together to achieve overriding goals which are real and compelling to all concerned."[52]

If only there was as much harmony and cooperation in America today—and if only our leaders displayed as much common sense and willingness to work with others as those eleven- and twelve-year-old boys. Sadly, in a world driven by zero-sum outcomes, in which there are no consolation prizes for the loser, common sense has been tossed out the window.

I'm not telling you to abandon your family and friends who make up your tribe. I'm simply encouraging you to step outside your comfort zone and talk to someone with opposing views. America would be a much better place if we truly got to know those people who might think, talk, and act differently from us.

If only Americans would sit around a campfire and pass around a talking stick today.

CHAPTER 6

We're Not That Different

Before I became mayor of Midland, Texas, I was very involved in educational matters at the local level. While at the state capitol of Texas in Austin, I was given the opportunity to visit with Lieutenant Governor Dan Patrick about educational funding. As soon as I sat down in Patrick's office, he asked me, "Reverend, are you going to sign my bathroom bill?"

In 2017, I don't believe many of us believed this issue would become the hot-button issue it has now become. Today, the issue has evaded common sense and become another battleground of the extremes. But at the time, I was already well down this Middle path—more concerned with who was seeking to understand before demanding to be understood.

Patrick championed a state law that would have forced school districts, public universities, and government buildings to adopt policies requiring multi-occupancy bathrooms and changing facilities to be designated and used only by people based on their biological sex. The law would have reversed local ordinances that allowed transgender people to use restrooms aligned with their gender identities. While on principle I agreed with the commonsense matter of who should use what bathroom, at the time, I was more concerned with how the debate was raging and how groups were being pitted against one another absent conversation and compassion.

Several politicians and conservative groups supported the bill. LGBTQ+ advocates and business owners, concerned the state's economy would be hurt by the discriminatory action, opposed it.

Patrick's question caught me completely off guard. I wasn't ready to have that discussion with him, but I did ask him, "Have you spent any time having a conversation with people on the other side? Do you have any gay friends or gay family members that you've had conversations with? Why don't you have those talks and call me? Then I'll tell you whether I'm going to sign your letter of support or not."

What bothered me most wasn't that we were so ideologically opposite about the issue, but how the entire episode seemed devoid of compassion. I had many friends and acquaintances who were gay, who wondered why they were getting lumped in with the transgender debate; they understood the reality of the issue but not the accusations of the debate. The extremes on both sides of the issue were the loudest, and the conversations and concerns that needed to take place among the majority middle were missing. I'm not sure any of us knew back in 2017 that this particular issue would escalate to the point we see today, but hindsight reminds me that in the midst of heated debates, we often miss the commonsense of the Middle and turn into warring tribes. Once again, it was one extreme or the other.

Patrick looked at me, speechless, as our conversation ground to a halt. He walked out of the room. His assistant came into the office to inform me that my time with him was up.

People living in the Middle understand that we have to go through life *with* others, not *through* them. We need to coexist with our neighbors, whether they live next door to us or on the other side of town. We have to figure out how to get along with others, regardless of their backgrounds and beliefs, and somehow strive to work together to make things work.

The Middle understands that if we continue down the path of viewing nearly every issue through the lens of extremes, we'll overlook the basic principles of being an American: It takes a village to accomplish most things, so we must meet in the middle. Standing on opposite sides and shouting obscenities and accusations at one another gets us nowhere. Life isn't a zero-sum game—it's a community game.

Sadly, many people living outside the Middle not only believe that the other side is wrong—they fear what the other side might do to our country's future. Academics refer to this distrust of the opposing party as "affective polarization." Stanford researcher Shanto Iyengar coined the term, noting that a new type of division has emerged in recent years: "Ordinary Americans increasingly dislike and distrust those from the other party. Democrats and Republicans both say that the other party's members are hypocritical, selfish, and closed-minded, and they are unwilling to participate across party lines."[53]

How are we supposed to get anywhere or make any progress if both sides view the other with equal disdain and skepticism?

In *The Coddling of the American Mind: How Good Intentions and Bad Ideas Are Setting Up a Generation for Failure,* authors Greg Lukianoff and Jonathan Haidt explained affective polarization another way:

> Identity can be mobilized in ways that emphasize an overarching common humanity while making the case that some fellow human beings are denied dignity and rights because they belong to a particular group, or it can be mobilized in ways that amplify our ancient tribalism and bind people together in shared hatred of a group that serves as the unifying common enemy.[54]

The sad truth is that, as tribalism has intensified in our country, many Americans fail to realize that people on the other side of the aisle may not be so different from themselves. We've been neatly put into endless groups like African Americans, Chinese Americans, West Texans, East Texans, liberals, conservatives, Republicans, Democrats, independents, and so on. It's time for America to reject the lazy mentality of categories, pull off—and look past—simple external labels, and work together toward the common good within our common humanity.

One of the reasons so many Americans have become blinded

by tribalism is that our view of the other side has been so distorted by extremism. In an 2024 Axios report, journalists Jim VandeHei and Mike Allen cited ample evidence suggesting that "we've been trapped in a reality distortion bubble—social media, cable TV, and tribal political wars—long enough to warp our view of the reality around us."[55]

While differing views exist in America on subjects such as abortion, immigration, and women's reproductive rights, the opinions on the extreme fringes have become the loudest voices on social media, certain cable TV networks, and among politicians who use them to their advantage.

Here's what the extremes are hiding from those of us in the Middle: A very small percentage of the wealthiest and most powerful people in America control the media outlets that feed us information they want us to hear and read. This control is accomplished through the modern tragedy of algorithms that feed us what stokes our animosity toward others. We are being fed distrust, distortion, and dislike. We must reprogram the algorithm of our own thinking if we are ever to revive our common American dream.

Making matters worse, the Ronald Reagan administration repealed the Fairness Doctrine in 1986—a policy that required broadcasters to give equal time to both sides of a political issue. This led to the launch of CNN, and then Fox News in 1996. Now, there's CNBC, MSNBC, NewsNation, and Newsmax TV, each of which inarguably leans to one side of the aisle in their political coverage, whether they want to admit it or not. While the intent of the Fairness Doctrine may have been good, the mere presence of the policy was an indication that we had either stopped practicing or completely forgotten the value and power of free speech that honors and listens to the other side.

Over the decades, these media outlets have done little to expand our conversation. One can hardly dispute that the opposite has happened, and we have hardened on the edges. At the same time, the media grows increasingly frustrated in its search for common decency, deliberation, and productivity for all.

In 2018, a group called More in Common, which works to build more united and inclusive democratic societies in the United States, United Kingdom, Poland, Germany, France, Spain, and Brazil, found that the wealthiest groups in America were "Devoted Conservatives" (6 percent) and "Progressive Activists" (8 percent) who dominate media, political parties, and higher education.[56]

More in Common's groundbreaking research found that "most Americans are tired of this 'us-versus-them' mindset and are eager to find common ground."[57]

"In talking to everyday Americans, we have found a large segment of the population whose voices are rarely heard above the shouts of the partisan tribes," the report said. "These are people who believe that Americans have more in common than that which divides them. While they differ on important issues, they feel exhausted by the division in the United States. They believe that compromise is necessary in politics, as in other parts of life, and want to see the country come together and solve its problems."[58]

We're Not That Different

More in Common found that America's differences have become "dangerously tribal, fueled by a culture of outrage and taking offense." The report continues:

> For the combatants, the other side can no longer be tolerated, and no price is too high to defeat them. . . . Once a country has become tribalized, debates about contested issues from immigration and trade to economic management, climate change and national security, become shaped by larger tribal identities. Policy debate gives way to tribal conflicts. Polarization and tribalism are self-reinforcing and will likely continue to accelerate.[59]

Our country's culture of outrage and taking offense has only been exacerbated in recent presidential elections—regardless of which side of the aisle won or lost. Presidents from both parties have added fuel to the fire through an endless array of jabs and barbs directed at the opposing party, demonstrating a lack of statesmanship and decorum that might otherwise elevate our common humanity and lead us to work together rather than divide us. Neither party is exempt. The opposing sides have only grown louder, larger, and less willing to move to the middle for our common good. In his book *Republic of Wrath: How American Politics Turned Tribal, from George Washington to Donald Trump,* Brown University professor of political science and public policy James A. Morone noted that the US has faced "darker times in the past" and experienced "worse violence and more blood."[60]

"But today's division ought to worry us," Morone wrote, "for they go deep. They are not simply about political preferences but about essential identity—about who we are and what Americans look like."[61]

America's political parties are not only defined by ideology and platforms but also, as Morone wrote, have now

> sorted themselves by race, nativism, and sexuality—tribal differences, intensified by a new media, that all reflects the most passionate divisions running through American history. The party differences have grown still hotter because the parties are evenly matched. The identity issues—whites on one side, people of color on the other—give the tight political competition a special intensity. Not only are they the "enemy" but they come from a visibly different tribe—and they could win it all in the next election.[62]

Believe it or not, a survey conducted by the Associated Press and NORC Center for Public Affairs Research in March 2024 found that most Americans actually agree on many issues affecting our country. In fact, more than 75 percent of the adults surveyed said equal protection under the law, the right to vote, freedom of speech, the right to privacy, freedom of religion, the right to assemble peacefully, and freedom of the press are important to America's identity.[63]

Maybe we're not all that different after all—at least not as much as those on the extremes and in the media would like us to believe.

"If you get a bunch of normal people at random and put them

in a room together and chat about issues, there's a lot more convergence than you might imagine," Michael Albertus, a political science professor at the University of Chicago, told the Associated Press.[64]

Those people on the extremes and polarization have shredded America to the point that we've lost faith in our elected leaders, we've lost trust in one another, and we no longer know who we are or where we fit in society.

Take any natural disaster or tragedy, and you will see just how connected we are. Through every hurricane or flood, plane crash or act of terror, we become galvanized across every race, creed, religion, sexual orientation, or political party. In the face of human hardship, no one asks politically charged questions. Instead, we gather together in our shared humanity and give one another a helping hand up and out of tragedy.

Sadly, after another twenty-four hours or so, politicians step in, and the blaming and scapegoating begin. Then the tragedy becomes a debate about climate change, or a government department is blamed because of its diversity, equity, and inclusion (DEI) or environmental, social, and governance (ESG) commitments. We'll soon hear that the federal government doesn't care about the poor citizens of a rural county or a state, or that a local government was too concerned about budgets or policy to act accordingly.

When it's all said and done, it's the Middle who rises to the occasion at the local level and makes a difference in the lives of their neighbors—fellow human beings not much different than themselves.

Years ago, while serving in South Sudan, I noticed that various humanitarian groups were drilling water wells for the poor. What caught my attention was how many denominations, religions, and interest groups were drilling wells in the same area for ostensibly the same reason—to help people in need. I started asking why we weren't pooling our resources for more effective results. I wasn't anticipating the answer I received: No one wanted to partner together because each group wanted credit for its own well, hoping to gain as many followers from the Sudanese as possible.

This was a glaring case of helping that often hurt. The need was so great you could attract any suffering human to your side by meeting their basic needs for survival. This was a classic bait and switch of a nature much like the rhetoric of all extremes in the current political climate in America.

The motive of the extremes on both sides of the aisle is to draw us away from rather than toward one another. This is a system and structure designed to accumulate followers and gain power. All sides of the extremes have this one thing in common—to separate us based on our differences rather than remember how much alike we are. We share basic human needs and desires. Though we will have our differences, we are indeed more alike than different. We have basic human needs that require provision. We all need and want love and compassion. We all need and want community. According to our basic founding documents, we are endowed with certain inalienable rights. We must commit on an individual level to fight for one another to obtain them as well, even through our differences.

Nearly two decades ago, I was invited to preach at a service honoring Dr. Martin Luther King. The topic of my sermon was "We Are All Racists." Not surprisingly, many in the audience were surprised by the topic. My message was clear: Any time we look at someone else and choose a negative definition of him or her based on race or appearance, we are being racist. The point was not to minimize our racial struggles—or the progress we've made and haven't made in America—but to remind those in the audience that we too often look first at differences through our personal paradigms. We would be far better off embracing a shared humanity that chooses to see we are not that different to begin with.

Back in 2017, the Texas legislature failed to take action on the bathroom bill, so Texas Governor Greg Abbott called a thirty-day special session to consider it. The bill died on the floor and never reached Abbott's desk.

A 2017 *Texas Tribune* and University of Texas poll found that the so-called bathroom bill was important to only 44 percent of the state's voters—and "very important" to only 26 percent.[65] Once again, those on the extreme screamed loud enough and often enough to transform a controversial issue into a partisan one, while the majority of citizens didn't think it was all that important to begin with.

CHAPTER 7

Losing the Core

During my tenure as senior pastor of Stonegate Fellowship, we went through a season in which a shocking number of marriages in the church ended in divorce. I turned to Dr. Kathy Koch, a close friend and the founder of Celebrate Kids in Dallas.

Dr. Koch had spent much of her career helping parents and educators raise kids who are confident and resilient. One of her core methods is what she calls our "Five Core Needs." I often refer to it as a pyramid effect, which proposes that a strong sense of identity positively impacts a child's competence, security, purpose, and sense of belonging. Dr. Koch became a dear friend, and as I listened and learned from her, I became convinced that her pyramid could help the couples in our church who were struggling in their marriages.

Security is the foundation of Dr. Koch's pyramid. We must ask ourselves: *Whom can I trust?* We must learn to trust God, of course, along with honest and dependable people—and ourselves. But we should never put our trust in power, popularity, or wealth. If a person's security is impaired because of trust issues, he or she won't know how to shape a healthy identity. When security and identity are flawed, a person struggles to understand where they belong, their purpose, and their competence. As a result, their talents will be hindered and put at risk because all these other factors have been compromised.

Dr. Koch came up with the idea that everyone goes through life each day asking five questions:

1. Whom can I trust?
2. Who am I?
3. Who wants me?
4. Why am I alive?
5. What do I do well?[66]

As I continued to study and apply Dr. Koch's Five Core Needs pyramid, I began to see that if someone's security, identity, belonging, and purpose have been threatened, their first response is often to guard, protect, defend, and blame. Eventually, they'll do something they later regret.

For example, when I was a pastor, a couple came to see me, seeking help for their struggling marriage. The husband told me, "I had an affair. I don't know how it happened. Our marriage just started falling apart."

I sat down across from him and asked, "Let me get this straight: Did you just wake up one day frustrated and go find another woman to sleep with?"

"Well, no, that's stupid," he said.

"So, this took time, correct?" I said. "I bet at some point you sat at work one day, and thought to yourself, *You know, I bet my wife's at home. She's been thinking about me all day, and when I get home, she's probably going to be naked and have the kids in bed and have sex with me immediately.*"

I told the man that I bet when he arrived at home, his wife had on sweatpants, their kids were screaming, and she said, "These are your kids. You need to handle them right now."

"What you wanted, what you imagined, and what you thought you deserved didn't happen," I told him. "You called into question if she really wanted you."

I continued, "And let's imagine that when you went in to work the next day, an attractive assistant who had recently been hired greeted you with a smile and said, 'Hey, Billy, looks like you've been working out.' She gave you the affirmation and interest you'd been wanting from your wife. After a few morning greetings like this, maybe your mind started to wander. Maybe you stopped by her desk for a chat a few times a day. Maybe you imagined what it would feel like to hold her. After a little while, maybe you jumped into bed with her. Later, when the affair was over, however, you realized there was still something big missing in your life."

In counseling couples through crisis, I always advised them that, unless they had a greater vision and purpose, they would never be able to fight their natural instincts to guard, protect, and defend themselves. For couples, the greater vision and purpose is one of love for each other that involves, but is not limited to, values such as sacrifice, compassion, and endurance. Long-standing couples see the greater purpose and vision that revolves around family and community, and is rarely about self and what one party to the marriage can get for themselves. Couples who see and pursue this greater purpose and vision for each other find that their personal sacrifice and commitment actually meets their needs above and beyond what any selfish pursuit could ever deliver. *All for one and one for all* isn't just a battle cry for musketeers—it works for marriages and countries as well.

In many ways, that's exactly how America is today. We don't have a greater vision or purpose. We don't trust one another. We don't trust our government. We don't know who we are as Americans. We don't even know if we belong to one another because of tribalism, affective polarization, and a media and political system that profit and benefit from our differences—no matter how small they might be.

Because we don't know what our purpose is as one nation—*indivisible with liberty and justice for all*—all we can do is go after what we want, what we see, and what we think we deserve. And, of course, we'll guard, protect, defend, and blame people and things around us, because our security, identity, belonging, and purpose are so out of whack.

In my opinion, America's most pressing problem is that it's lost its greater vision and purpose as a country. Our nation was at its strongest when we worked together toward a collective goal. There have been profound moments in our history when it happened, starting with the American Revolution, when the colonies rallied together to end British rule and establish one of the first modern democracies with elected representatives and a written constitution. Much of America came together again under President Abraham Lincoln's leadership during the Civil War to preserve the Union and abolish slavery.

Perhaps at no time did the United States show its collective force more than when its citizens rallied together to fight Nazi Germany and the Axis powers during World War II. About 16.1 million Americans enlisted in the armed forces during the war, including about 407,000 who never made it back.[67]

At home, American factories were transformed into producers of tanks, planes, ships, weapons, and ammunition. With millions of men fighting overseas, women left their homes and went to work in factories, shipyards, and offices. "Rosie the Riveter," an iconic poster of a female factory worker flexing her muscles, became the lasting image of female strength and patriotism. Citizens rationed food, gasoline, rubber, and other essential goods to support the war effort, and families grew victory gardens to supplement rations and boost morale.

Perhaps the most famous call to action by an American president came from John F. Kennedy during his "Moonshot Speech" at Rice University in Houston, Texas, on September 12, 1962. With the Russians having already launched the first satellite (Sputnik) and sent the first astronaut, Yuri Gagarin, into space, Kennedy challenged the nation to land a man on the Moon before the end of the decade.

"We choose to go to the Moon," President Kennedy said that day. "We choose to go to the Moon in this decade and do the other things, not because they are easy, but because they are hard, because that goal will serve to organize and measure the best of our energies and skills, because that challenge is one that we are willing to accept, one we are unwilling to postpone, and one which we intend to win, and the others, too."[68]

Inspired by JFK's speech, Americans worked together to pursue what seemed impossible at the time—to explore the next great frontier and send a man to the Moon. "We set sail on this new sea because there is new knowledge to be gained, and new rights to be won, and they must be won and used for the progress of all people," Kennedy said.[69]

On July 20, 1969, President Kennedy's dream came to fruition when astronauts Neil Armstrong and Buzz Aldrin landed on the Moon during the Apollo 11 mission.

President Kennedy's leadership gave us a greater vision that united us. Today, we as a nation desperately need a new "Moonshot" vision that will help us begin to trust one another again, because our confidence in one another and the government is near an all-time low. If the country's collective faith is in shambles, the people's identity as Americans is ruined, as is our belonging to a shared community. We can no longer pursue our purpose as a country. If these important characteristics are missing from the core of who we are, we will never get back to the nation we were supposed to be.

In her book *Five to Thrive*, Dr. Koch offered what I believe is a more spiritual and refined interpretation of American psychologist Abraham Maslow's "Hierarchy of Needs," a theory that describes five levels of need that motivate, animate, and often dictate human behavior, actions, and responses to nature.[70]

Without a doubt, there's ample evidence that America has strayed from four of these five essential needs, thus impacting the daily lives of those living in the Middle. If nothing else, our current situation should cause us to consider whether the Middle can get back to addressing our essential needs and move away from the self-centered and power-driven behaviors often seen at the extremes.

For our purposes, I'm going to focus on four of Dr. Koch's needs that I believe apply to the current predicament in America. These four core needs, in descending order of their individual and collective importance, are as follows:

Core Need #1: Security

Security is the biggest foundational core need that is affecting America today. It revolves around the question, Who can I trust? In our case, we might say, Who can *we* trust?

For decades, Americans had an unwavering confidence in the government, elected officials, media, and the basic tenets of American values. Even during periods of significant social unrest, that cornerstone of protection seemed unshakable in the American experiment and way of life.

It is undeniable that individual and collective trust in our country has been on the decline for decades. This trust probably began eroding in the sixties, when tens of thousands of US soldiers were being killed in Vietnam in a war the American people didn't understand. Following the Tet Offensive of January 1968, many Americans began to question the government's claims that we were winning the war. When it was revealed that US soldiers killed hundreds of unarmed Vietnamese civilians, including women and children, in the Mai Lai massacre in March 1968, the nation faced a moral reckoning over Americans' conduct in the war.

High-profile political assassinations in the sixties only increased the public's distrust in government. President Kennedy was shot and killed while riding in a motorcade in Dallas, Texas, on November 22, 1963. Immediately, there were questions about whether his killer, Lee Harvey Oswald, acted alone, leading to conspiracy theories that are still alive today.

On February 21, 1965, three members of the Nation of Islam gunned down civil rights leader Malcolm X in the Audubon Ballroom in New York.

Then, tragically, civil rights leader Martin Luther King Jr. was shot and killed on April 4, 1968, while standing on a balcony of the Lorraine Motel in Memphis, Tennessee. His death sparked nationwide protests and riots.

Only three months later, US presidential candidate Robert F. Kennedy, JFK's brother, was assassinated during a primary victory speech at the Ambassador Hotel in Los Angeles on June 5, 1968, furthering America's disillusionment and distrust of the establishment.

America's individual and collective trust continued to crumble with each passing decade. Racial tensions of the late 1960s and 1970s, the Watergate scandal that led to President Richard Nixon's resignation in 1974, and social movements like women's rights and feminism—that sparked the Supreme Court's landmark *Roe v. Wade* decision that legalized abortion in 1973—each chipped away at public trust. The HIV/AIDS epidemic of the 1980s, along with economic crises such as inflation, high unemployment, slow economic growth, and income inequality, all led to an inherited suspicion of leaders, fueled by extreme perspectives.[71]

In the past decade, racial and social justice movements like Black Lives Matter, gun violence and mass shootings, climate change, the COVID-19 epidemic, the ongoing opioid crisis, immigration and border security, and foreign concerns—including Russia's invasion of Ukraine and the Israel-Hamas war—have sparked heated debates and left many Americans wondering which side to trust.

With political polarization and tribalism reaching unprecedented extremes this past decade, the Middle realizes this erosion of confidence is eating away at our core, and we must somehow restore it—quickly. We have become protective and defensive of trust rather than beginning with trust. We have allowed that lack of trust to become our default.

When we think about our other relationships, we know that everything is affected when trust has been violated. When children learn early on not to trust parents or friends, this critical need for security taints every other internal thought process they have. Over the past several decades, politics and religion at the highest levels of leadership have violated the people's trust. Whether because of broken promises, mismanaged national events, perceived deception, or abuse of power, the populace has little faith in the establishment they were raised to trust.

America's faith in media is also at an all-time low, no matter which direction we choose to look. Over the past quarter century, the American people have watched the media take sides—not only on policy but regarding people as well. Media personalities refer to one side or the other in pejorative terms and labels that do nothing but drive a deeper wedge between people, violating the sacred trust people should be able to place in the media. Sadly, the days of objective news are over; it's now a twenty-four-hour cycle of continuous spin and hyperbole.

When the foundation of trust is cracked, all other essential needs and actions lack a solid footing. When our security and trust are broken, we don't know who to listen to or what to believe about our personal identity and belonging, not to mention our ultimate purpose. When this happens, people will easily gravitate to extreme claims that seem to be a secure pathway to something or someone to trust. Rather than trust built on the ideals of a common America and its values, we divide even further, seeking individual and group forms of identity we think will give us the foundation we want.

Core Need #2: Identity

The second core need of Dr. Koch's pyramid, identity, raises the question, Who am I? or, more precisely, Who are we? It has become increasingly common among academic and political elites to promote the idea that the traditional perception of America as a "city set on a hill" no longer exists, suggesting instead that our country has a deeply flawed and troubling history.

The Middle has watched as various parts of American identity have been either co-opted or criticized by both the radical left and the reactive right. The Middle recognizes that this polarization has caused many people to feel that something essential about who and what we are as a nation has been lost amid divisive rhetoric and the demonization of the "other side" by the extremes.

Because security and trust have been so deeply damaged, we no longer know where to go for affirmation—of our personal identity or of our collective national identity. Consequently, we leave the definition of our identity to the vicissitudes of the extremes that seem so certain and confident. This is why cults of both a secular and religious nature find such ardent followings. Individuals with broken security and missing identity are drawn to those who live and teach on the extremes. It allows false leaders to divide their followers from families, friends, and others.

We have become a collective of people lacking individual trust and security, so instead we find false security and misplaced identity in the perceived certainty and comfort of the extremes seeking to control us. Rather than identifying first as Americans, we allow the extremes on both sides to capitalize on what divides us rather than on what unites us. We have tribalized ourselves based on race, religion, creed, gender, and the like in vain attempts to find security and a sense of identity.

The founding of this great nation was built on the trust that we could self-govern, and we could trust one another in our shared identity as Americans from all races, religions, creeds, and nationalities. The pride of being an American was of such great value that immigrants from around the world risked their lives to come to the US.

Today, there is no clear understanding of what it means to be an American. Religious extremists decide who is a "real" Christian or person of faith, while political and cultural police determine who counts as a true patriot. Consequently, we have lost the identity that once bound us together, which was built on a mutual trust that grounds us.

Core Need #3: A Sense of Belonging

Once security and trust have been compromised and identity has been lost, it doesn't take long for people to lose their sense of belonging, which is Koch's third core need. Belonging asks the question, Who wants me? This need has historically been found in family and community relations, and through mutual commitment to a cause greater than any one individual and shared by many. Belonging has been found in difficult relationships, where trust is built, identity is forged, and the bonds of community are strengthened not only by what we agree on but also by what we learn from one another in our disagreements.

At the heart of this question is a deep desire to be part of something important and affirming. For decades, simply being an American was a significant part of one's identity—and often the part that mattered most. Being an American was the dream of millions of people who have traveled from all over the world to become US citizens. However, the extremes have once again driven wedges of division into our collective identity and belonging, leaving the Middle feeling disconnected and uncertain about its place and value. Those in the Middle are left feeling not much of anything when it comes to identity and belonging.

The Middle wonders what happened to the great value of belonging to this great nation. We wonder what happened to belonging to a nation that, despite being composed of a myriad of viewpoints, still respects one another and seeks solutions and answers for the greater good.

Core Need #4: Purpose

Purpose, Dr. Koch's fourth core need, explores the question, What is our purpose on this earth? Throughout much of America's history, our collective purpose was clear and abiding in the pursuit of life, liberty, and happiness. This motive was rooted in the ideal of a nation where free individuals lived and worked together to create the best possible life for themselves and their communities.

Our collective objective embodied the values of the land of the free and the home of the brave—warts and all. However, these days, this sense of purpose has evaporated, leaving us with partisan extremism that seems hell-bent on driving us apart and making enemies of one another. The Middle is left pondering where the overarching purpose of the American dream went—a purpose that once inspired and united so many people, both domestically and globally, and made America the envy and rescuer of the world.

The greater purpose and calling of America—to serve as a beacon of democracy and the responsibility to live toward one another with respect and honor—seem to have been lost, if not forgotten. At some point, we must begin the process of rebuilding trust in one another and in our institutions and leadership. This will begin only when we have a revival of servant leadership toward our neighbor and from those who desire to carry the mantle of leadership.

Author Stephen Covey described this troubling cultural shift as

> an increasing venomous tone . . . creeping into . . . our non-communication. We seem to be at an all-time low for civility in discourse. There's anger, division, frustration, and polarization. Even at the highest levels of government, where mutual respect once reigned, we hear time and again of outbursts instead of dialogue. . . . On the internet, on cable TV's so-called news, on the radio waves of every nation, demagogues have found a shortcut to wealth by cheering and cursing people into opposing camps.[72]

But this national security issue of low trust, a resultant lack of a common identity and belonging, and the loss of our greater purpose will begin to change for the better only when we as individuals face our own security, identity, belonging, and purpose challenges.

The entire issue boils down to a choice to rebuild national trust so we can rebuild our shared American identity, belonging, and historical purpose. This restoration of trust will require deep personal and collective searching at many levels. We must recover our shared identity as Americans of all stripes and reenter our diverse communities by belonging to something bigger than ourselves.

A couple of hours after President Ronald Reagan was shot in the left side by a would-be assassin at the Washington Hilton hotel on March 30, 1981, he was about to undergo surgery to remove a bullet that stopped an inch from his heart.

Before an anesthesiologist put Reagan under, he joked to his surgeons: "I hope you are all Republicans."[73]

Dr. Joseph Giordano, a liberal Democrat, told Reagan: "Today, Mr. President, we are all Republicans."[74]

Americans of all colors, political leanings, and backgrounds rallied behind a president who had been in his first term for only seventy days when he was nearly killed. They didn't see a Republican or Democrat or liberal or conservative, but a leader who handled a crisis with dignity and grace.

Reagan, who lost half his blood that day, spent thirteen days in the hospital before returning to the White House. In a diary entry on April 14, 1982, President Reagan wrote, "I'm more and more convinced that Americans are hungering to feel proud and patriotic again."[75]

If only it could feel like that in America again.

CHAPTER 8

Leaderless

American author and pastor John Maxwell has often reminded us that everything rises and falls on leadership. If this is true—and I believe it is—then the rancor, extremism, division, and disrespect so common in our nation must have found its example in leadership.

Or, as the saying goes: As the leaders go, so go the people.

Jesus of Nazareth put it this way to His followers: "You are the salt of the earth, but if salt has lost its taste, how shall its saltiness be restored? It is no longer good for anything except to be thrown out and trampled under people's feet" (Matthew 5:13).

The point of both Maxwell and Jesus (not to equate the two!) is that the purpose of leadership—and of salt—is to benefit those influenced by its properties and example. Those watching and following will get the message of what behavior is good or bad to imitate from their leaders. If we are a nation divided by extremes, it is because of the example of its so-called leaders.

The Middle

In a 2024 Gallup poll, respondents were asked to list their top "unprompted" concerns facing the nation. Participants in this open-ended poll weren't given a list of suggested issues; instead, they were asked to rank concerns that mattered most to them on their own. The results might surprise you: After immigration, approximately 20 percent of respondents cited government/poor leadership as the most significant problem facing America today. Remarkably, lack of leadership ranked ahead of the economy, inflation, poverty, crime, race relations, abortion, unemployment, and the ongoing conflict in the Middle East.[76]

Effective leadership sets a country's vision, galvanizes its mission, and unifies its people to pursue objectives for the greater good. On the other hand, tyranny arises when so-called leaders impose their own agenda and compel people to serve their personal interests. America was founded on the guiding principles of radical freedom and liberty, where, as stated throughout this book, each is free to pursue life, liberty, and happiness in their own way, provided they do no harm to others and adhere to the rule of law.

What has been lacking in America for too long is effective leadership that promotes a vision greater than simply defeating the other side. In the Middle, there is a profound desire for a vision that unites people around the greater good rather than rallying the troops to undermine the opposition and remove them from power. This deficiency in leadership pervades not only government but also religion, academia, media, and everyday life on Main Street.

The Middle recalls the selfless leadership of great men and women throughout American history. They remember the lessons from history books about George Washington dismissing the idea that he could be made a king in America, instead believing in the true cause of American liberty. They recall Abraham Lincoln's humility in building a cabinet of his political opponents—the famous "team of rivals"—to restore a nation that relied on unity from both sides.

As noted in the previous chapter, those in the Middle also remember John F. Kennedy's inspiring words about choosing to go to the Moon and tackle other challenges, "not because they are easy, but because they are hard."[77] This kind of "Moonshot" leadership created a sense of unity in America that helped solve many societal problems in the 1960s.

The Middle witnessed how quickly Americans could unite and meet in the compassionate middle in the face of unimaginable tragedy on September 11, 2001. In the weeks and months following terrorist attacks in New York and Washington, DC, people set aside their differences—even those on the extremes—for common good. They worked together to rescue survivors, provide aid, and start the process of rebuilding our nation. It was much the same when the world was confronted with the COVID-19 pandemic not long ago, although politics soon infected the good many were trying to do.

During my tenure as a mayor of Midland, Texas, I knew I was positioned squarely in the healthy middle because people from both sides often disagreed with my decisions. The supportive emails and letters I received after numerous appearances on CNN, Fox News, BBC, and other media outlets affirmed to me that the Middle wanted a leader who represented them rather than one who catered to the loudest and most extreme voices on the fringes.

The Middle

While appearing on various network interviews, I was asked about energy and climate. On most occasions, I would simply respond with the great West Texas mindset that we were for energy and could not understand why there was such demonization related to oil and gas and a lack of conversation about energy.

After every network interview, I received emails and text messages from people literally around the world saying, "I probably disagree with you on many political matters, but I agree with you that we have lost the ability to have important and necessary conversations." These responses from around the globe began to form in me a conviction that there is a silent middle majority out there longing for reasonable and respectful leadership right down the middle.

It is a well-known axiom in the political world that you campaign to win and legislate to stay in office. It's how the machinery works in state and national politics, even more so than in local government. Even when campaign season rolls around every two, four, or six years, elected politicians often blame everyone else for their inability to get anything done, get reelected to office, and repeat the process all over again. The system determines the behavior. The only way to fix this perpetuation of the extremes is term limits and the removal of the "gain mechanism" for elected officeholders.

We need selfless leaders who are in office to serve. As mayor of Midland, I was paid $75 a month. I oversaw the municipal government of the most important oil and gas city in the country, home to the most abundant and secure oil and gas supply in the world. And yet the only incentive for me to be in office was to serve. Honestly, it was costing me more money to be in office than what I was earning in my monthly stipend. This type of service mandate changes the way you think about everything because it keeps you grounded in everyday life as you run your business and serve the city. We need a return to this sacrificial service at a national level.

The Middle has witnessed and recalled from our history what genuine and effective leadership looks like at the local, state, and national levels. They remember when leaders pulled everyone together toward the center, fostering a shared journey rather than shouting at one another from the extremes.

Today, we are surrounded by voices and talking heads who do little more than denigrate one another or the other side of the political divide. Even the ubiquitous "Make America Great Again" call of President Donald Trump is often met with criticism that "we are not great because of the other side," while Democrats decry the MAGA group as a "bunch of fascists."

The majority in the Middle longs for the leadership that calls individuals back to their greatness—found in the pursuit of something bigger than themselves and something bigger than bitter partisan bickering back and forth of the left and right. Our current environment is marked by bombastic sound bites from spokespersons and pied pipers on both sides, while the Middle is waiting for both sides to be quiet. The Middle is longing for a greater vision for the entirety of the nation to emerge rather than one that is constructed to simply defeat the other side.

The Indian lawyer and social activist Mahatma Gandhi believed that the following seven "social sins" would destroy society:

wealth without work, pleasure without conscience, knowledge without character, commerce without morality, science without humanity, religion without sacrifice, and politics without principle.[78] Gandhi, the leader of the Indian Independence Movement against British rule and widely remembered for his philosophy of nonviolent resistance, published this list in his weekly newsletter, *Young India*, in 1925. He gave a copy of the list to his grandson, Arun Gandhi, shortly before his assassination on January 30, 1948.

The principles of respect and honor for one another that Gandhi and other world leaders championed long ago have been lost in our society.

The driving principle of American politics seems to be to win at all costs. Executive orders have a long history in the United States for myriad reasons. In our current leadership vacuum, our Congress moves from continuing resolution to continuing resolution, while important societal issues—immigration, crime, sexuality, abortion, and more—are left to be decided by executive orders. These decisions are then exacerbated by the extremes and often overturned by an executive order from the next administration.

The point in all this is that leadership is supposed to elevate debate and discourse, so critical issues can be debated and resolved. Our nation lacks the vision and leadership to engage in these difficult discussions because the extremes have divided us so much that there is little courage left in Washington, DC, to step out and change the discussion.

When we look at Gandhi's seven "social sins," we are reminded that attitude and actions reflect leadership. Is it any wonder we have descended into a blame-and-defend culture when we review Gandhi's list and realize those sins are playing out in the highest levels of leadership every day in our country?

Though we may not have committed the unpardonable sin in all seven categories, we can see where extremes have especially promoted:

- **Wealth Without Work:** Our political leaders jockey back and forth with historical entitlements with little to no discussion about how to fix the problem. Our supposed leaders have PhDs and master's degrees but no real work or life experience that matches the everyday American who lives and works in the majority middle.

- **Commerce Without Morality:** The issues of the environment, social matters, and governance should not be extreme matters. The majority middle understands the importance of wise stewardship of the environment, social matters, and governance. But when trust in the government is at an all-time low, and the extremes seize good ideas and use them for their own gain, that reasonable good is turned into the extreme debate, and the entire nation loses.

- **Science Without Humanity:** Who can forget the lack of leadership in America in the face of the COVID-19 pandemic? In the midst of fear and a worldwide epidemic that killed millions of people, the extremes in our country took hold of seemingly every issue related to vaccines, mask mandates, workplace and school shutdowns, and supply chain problems. Americans already had little trust in the government and media, and misinformation and conspiracy theories on social media about the virus, vaccines, and treatments led to hesitancy and distrust in public health institutions.

I was only a few weeks into my term as the Midland mayor when news started spreading about the COVID-19 pandemic that started in China and quickly spread around the world. On March 11, 2020, Dr. Anthony Fauci testified before Congress that the outbreak in America would get worse, and the same day the World Health Organization declared COVID-19 a pandemic. By the end of the night, fear was spreading like wildfire.

One of my customs when I'm traveling alone for work is to sit at a hotel bar or local establishment and watch a game on TV. That night, I was watching an Oklahoma Thunder basketball game when I noticed officials were stopping the game. The sound was off, so I wasn't sure exactly what was happening. People came in the restaurant and told me that the National Basketball Association suspended its season after a player tested positive for the virus. Other sports would soon do the same.

Four days later, New York City closed its public school system, and other cities and states would soon follow. Within a few weeks, there were government mandates to close schools and businesses, and all of us were soon confined to our homes with seemingly no end in sight.

Before I go into details of how I handled the COVID-19 crisis as mayor, I'll remind you that Midland is one of the reddest and most conservative cities in the country. The first meeting I had was with a group of doctors and nurses. They sat in my conference room and told me, "If you don't shut this city down, you're going to have two thousand dead people on your hands, and you better buy refrigerated trucks." At the time, bigger cities like Dallas and San Antonio had already issued shelter-in-place and mask mandates. I had been reading some of those shelter-in-place ordinances, and to be honest, they seemed kind of nutty.

The next meeting I had was with a group of business leaders from Midland. They told me, "If you shut the city down, you're a communist and a socialist Marxist, and we're going to make sure you get run out of office."

So, as I pondered what to do, I realized I had two options, and neither of them was in the middle. Texas Governor Greg Abbott had issued a statewide mask mandate, but I told our police department not to enforce it. "We're going to leave it up to the people," I told our officers.

As I was driving home from that second meeting, I listened to a news-talk radio host referring to me as the "freedom-loving mayor of Midland." Of course, I was going to listen to someone who thinks I'm great. Later, he found out that I had a mask mandate on the agenda for the next city council meeting. Now, he was lambasting me on the radio. I decided to call him.

"Hey, this is the mayor of Midland, Texas," I said. "If you love this country the way you say you love this country, I think you'll agree that, because we're built on freedom and representative republicanism, the best thing for me to do is to put it on the agenda for the council rather than issue a mask mandate."

Fox News learned about Midland's mayor not enforcing the governor's mask mandate, and someone reached out for me to appear on TV. The Fox News anchor said, "We hear you're picking a fight with the Texas governor."

"I'm not picking a fight with the governor," I explained. "What I have said publicly is that the governor needs to call the legislature together and stop issuing mandates that are lasting for months at a time. We're a representative republic, so let's act like it and legislate these issues. Let's not do executive orders."

About twenty minutes after my interview on Fox News, I received a phone call from someone close to the governor's office, who asked, "Why are you picking a fight with the governor?"

What happened to our ability to simply talk to one another and work things out? During the COVID-19 pandemic, much of what was being discussed was nothing more than fear-mongering. There was so much misinformation out there about masks, vaccines, and how the virus was transmitted, among other things.

To get on top of the important issue, I started hosting weekly fireside chats on Facebook from my living room. I sat in my chair and spent about an hour letting our citizens know what was happening with COVID-19: how many people were in the hospital, how many people had died, explaining the vaccine options, and encouraging people to consult with their doctor. I tried to take a path right down the middle, ignoring the loudest voices on the extremes. I encouraged people to take care of their neighbors, talk to their doctors, and make the best decisions for themselves when it came to masks and vaccines. For most of those chats, there were forty to fifty thousand people watching them within thirty-six hours.

Former US President Ronald Reagan once said, "The greatest leader is not necessarily the one who does the greatest things. He is the one that gets the people to do the greatest things."[79]

If only there were more men and women in leadership positions today to bring America back together to do great things again.

CHAPTER 9

Beans and Cornbread

When my kids were younger, I'd offer them words of encouragement as they left the house for school each morning. I'd tell each one of them, "You can be right, but you may not be wise." Other times, it was the more succinct, "Be wise," as they walked out the door.

Eventually, someone brought me a rock with the words "Be Wise" etched in it. It still sits at our front door.

If you're frustrated by the vitriol you're hearing from both sides of the political aisle, by the constant shouting and finger-pointing from pundits on TV news and social media, and if you're wondering what you can do to improve political discourse in America, I suggest that it all starts at home around the dinner table.

Many of us remember being told as children what subjects were off-limits around the holiday dinner table. It might be a question about where your favorite crazy uncle was this year, your cousin's new girlfriend, or which team lost the heated in-state football rivalry. Or maybe it was the old, classic warning, "Whatever you do, don't bring up politics!"

Those topics were considered taboo because there was a good chance that someone in the family was a die-hard Republican and another was a longtime Democrat. If someone brought up the recent election or hot-button political debate, everyone knew it would end up being a long night of heated opinions and pointed insults about Republican and Democratic policies. There would be shouting and screaming, and someone would inevitably end up storming out of the house in fury. Hopefully, everyone came back together over a Pabst Blue Ribbon in the end, and divisive issues gave way to family respect.

Unfortunately, over time, politics became even more personal and more extreme as the religious right and Republicans merged and Democrats were supposedly against everything good and righteous. However, something began to change as soon as the extreme right decided during the 1990s that Democrat Bill Clinton could not possibly be God's man for president. Two terms later, the political class came to blows like never before over hanging chads in Florida in the 2000 presidential election. After more than a month of chaos, following premature declarations of victories for both Democratic candidate Al Gore and Republican George W. Bush, multiple recounts, lawsuits, and Supreme Court decisions, Gore finally conceded to Bush (again) during a speech on national TV. Bush defeated Gore in Florida by fewer than six hundred votes out of almost six million cast, giving him enough Electoral College votes to succeed Clinton. An entire nation witnessed the blow-by-blow developments of an election bitterly divided—and eventually decided by attorneys and judges.

During the weeks the 2000 presidential election was in dispute, the radical left and reactive right had embarked on new territory, and gentlemen's behavior and the sacredness of a presidential election were tossed out the window, possibly forever.

The divide and vitriol only accelerated as Democrat Barack Obama arrived on the national political scene. Many on the reactive right predicted it would be the "end of America" if the first Black man were elected president, while the left accused the right of being unredeemable racists who only wanted to return to the Jim Crow era.

Making matters worse, the arrival of social media around this time transformed the twenty-four-hour news cycle into twenty-four-hour punditry. Instead of reasonable, polite discussions about important matters, angry, argumentative, and charged debates between multiple hosts became the norm. The beat continued through Supreme Court nominations, legislative gamesmanship, health care debates, and immigration over the past two decades.

As the early twenty-first century progressed, we moved into a new era in which we were connected by iPhones, the Internet, and social media, where opinions could be aired in real time. Respectful, face-to-face debate was thrown out in favor of keyboard warriors and faceless extremists.

Perhaps no single event in the past sixty years has demonstrated the chasm between the extreme left and far right more than the political rise of New York businessman Donald Trump and his presidential races against Hillary Clinton, Joe Biden, and Kamala Harris. Trump's bombastic leadership style while in office, and his not-so-peaceful exit from the White House after losing to Biden in 2020, were events never before seen in America.

The point of this chapter isn't to take sides with Trump—or anyone else—but to lament how those in the Middle have been blindsided by extremes for so long that the divide is so pronounced many don't even talk to their family and friends anymore. When I pitched this book idea at a convention of publishers, one man cried while telling me about the dear friends he'd lost over disagreements about Trump. He's not alone. Increasingly, Americans prefer to socialize and live with people who share their political views. A 2021 survey by the American Enterprise Institute found that 15 percent of American adults have ended a relationship over political differences.[80] Another study found 72 percent of Republican respondents were married to people from the same political party, and only 6 percent were married to Democrats. Likewise, 75 percent of Democrats were married to Democrats, and only 6 percent were married to a Republican.[81]

A 2017 study by Wakefield Research following Trump's first presidential victory over Hillary Clinton reported that 11 percent of respondents said, "differing politics have doomed a relationship," while that figure doubled for younger people. Another 29 percent said "the current political environment" had a negative impact on their relationship. Most shockingly, one-third of all married people in the survey said they would consider "getting a divorce if their spouse supported Trump."[82]

Those in the Middle have been left in disbelief that families and friends avoid one another because of animosity that is rooted in the collective soap opera of our current state of politics.

Another problem in America is that most families don't even eat dinner together very often. A 2022 report by the Survey Center of American Life found that only 38 percent of Gen Zers—young adults and teenagers born between the mid-1990s and mid-2010s—reported that their families ate together regularly while they were growing up. Conversely, more than 70 percent of Americans aged fifty or older said "they had family meals together every day during childhood."[83]

Previous studies found that students in sixth through twelfth grade who ate five to seven family dinners per week had "significantly lower odds of engaging in a number of high risk behavior patterns such as alcohol, drug, and tobacco use, depression-suicide, violence, antisocial behavior, and school problems when compared to those who typically ate zero to one dinners."[84] "Family meals may provide connection to important family and cultural rituals, which may in turn be beneficial for children's psychological functioning," another study found. "In addition, shared family meals may provide increased opportunities for communication and monitoring that may be related to a young person's opportunity or inclination to engage in risky or harmful behavior."[85]

It seems the pushback over politics at family dinners may have started years ago, when baby boomers in the 1960s came home from college with different views than they were raised with. Back then, most families agreed not to bring up certain topics anymore—or at least skip discussing the latest episode of *All in the Family*. But, through the decades, and even more in our day, it seems even our politics is dividing the family.

Upon closer examination, I've come to believe this is a reflection of the family more than our politics. For the past few decades, we've witnessed an erosion of public respect that has been amplified by the onslaught of twenty-four-hour news and the uncontrolled invasion of social media into our collective conscience.

Even in our homes, we have too often fallen prey to what divides us rather than what unites us. We have allowed conversations to take root that condemn those we don't know. We have reinforced divisions through families gathering around TVs to watch Fox News or CNN rather than gathering around the table to discuss the greatness of America, our shared humanity, and how this nation has found ways to come together in our hours of desperate need.

While discussing politics at home might have been taboo in the past, I believe it's the most fertile ground for exploring American values and discovering better solutions. Perhaps the revival of the Middle begins with parents from both sides of the aisle recommitting to lead by example, with conduct and speech that uplift others before seeking to divide them.

I believe my convictions on these matters—and the importance of discussion—came from my days in high school. I went to a predominantly white high school, and most of my close friends of color came through my time on the football team. Many of my

Black friends were attending this private school on scholarship—just like me. Being the only one with a car, I often picked them up for early summer practices or took them home. During these rides, I saw what you might call the "harder side of life." I didn't grow up rich, but their lives were certainly more difficult than mine. Around the dinner table with my mother, and sometimes with my best friend's family, I was taught there was more that binds us than divides us. I was raised to resist the seeds of the extremes because adults around the dinner table and in the living room were showing me by words and actions that we share a common humanity with everyone.

Growing up in Tulsa, Oklahoma, two of the most influential people in my life were Dan and JoEllen Quinten, the parents of my best friend, Lindy, who was the best man in my wedding. I met them in the fifth grade. On Thursday and Friday nights, everyone went to their house to watch movies. Lindy and I didn't attend the same high school, and since I was going to the private school across town that was close to their home, Dan gave me a key so I could eat lunch there.

A longtime train engineer, Dan was the kind of guy who was nice to everybody. He wouldn't say a negative word about anyone. Dan had a calm demeanor about everything. If I got in trouble, regardless of the decisions I made, he was there for me. Jody's hobby was ceramics, and each year after football or basketball season, she gave every one of us a figurine with our jersey number.

Since I lived in a single-parent home, Dan was a father figure to me. My mother had two jobs, working all day as a secretary and cleaning offices at night. I ate dinner with the Quintens a few nights every week. When Lindy and I came home on Friday nights, sometimes masking the smell of beer with mustard from the fridge when we were in college, Dan stayed up and talked with us about the issues and struggles we were dealing with. Those conversations often happened over a plate of leftover barbeque beans and cornbread.

While I was pastoring in Midland, Texas, my mother called me to tell me that they'd taken Dan to the hospital. They were afraid he wasn't going to make it. I jumped on a plane to Tulsa. When I arrived at the hospital, everyone else left the room. I leaned into Dan's ear and told him, "Thank you for changing my life. Thank you for teaching me to be a man."

Dan died on March 27, 2012. He was seventy-two years old. Dan and JoEllen were amazing examples of how to love and respect others.

There has never been a better time for parents and other reasonable adults to reclaim the conversations our children are hearing and having. The Middle longs for a return to the family discussions about football and the best new shows on Netflix instead of constant bickering and complaining about Trump, Democrats, and Republicans. We've lost our political moral compass as a nation, and the majority middle needs to lead the way back from the edges and into the synergy of better paths forward together.

It's probably prudent to talk to your children, if they're old enough, about politics and the government, as long as you're having respectful and reasonable conversations with them—and not the screaming matches they're watching on TV and social media. Having these talks with young people will allow them to learn to articulate where they stand on important issues, how to develop and defend their stance, and how to respectfully disagree with someone who might think differently than them. Talk to them about what you believe and why, and ask them how they feel about certain issues. Teach them to discern facts from fiction and to understand that not everything they see or hear on the TV news or social media is real. Explain to them that it's reasonable if one of their close friends feels differently about an important issue and that he or she doesn't have to end the relationship because they're on opposite sides.

Not one national poll reports the overwhelming support of the American people for anyone in government or religion. One after the other, politicians and religious leaders say one thing and do another. Whether it's issues concerning public policy or basic morals, the repetition of this vacuous public display of incompetence and power-grabbing leaves rubble and wreckage behind. The majority middle realizes the common denominator behind this Kabuki theater of our modern extremes is the radical left and right.

Now, classic liberals are dusting off their tweed coats with elbow patches, while old-school Republicans are donning their classic loafers, trousers, and blazers—longing for the good old days when politicians of both sides could be seen dining with one another. Instead of politicians who appear on TV in embarrassing sessions in which they're seemingly trying to say the worst possible thing about the other side, they want elected officials who will work toward middle ground.

Perhaps it's time for the majority middle to reclaim the family discussion. Turn off social media and news at home in the evening. Talk to your children about politics and, more importantly, how to serve others. Rather than avoiding these conversations at the table, we can find hope through conversations like those with our children.

We must choose to befriend and serve those different than ourselves and must collectively as families pull our children and the next generation back from the extremes that so easily galvanize us. Teach your children to be wise, to have good principles, and to make prudent decisions so they can honor others and serve greater causes.

It's time for America to have a little more wisdom . . . and a lot less rhetoric.

CHAPTER 10

Choose Service over Privilege

Believe it or not, leadership is not defined by who has the most followers and likes on social media or who screams the loudest but rather by who will give their life away for the good of others.

Robert K. Greenleaf was the founder of the modern servant leadership movement. A longtime executive at AT&T, Greenleaf studied management, education, and development for the communications company. After reading Herman Hesse's book, *Journey to the East*, the idea of servant leadership came to Greenleaf. He was worried about the authoritarian leadership style that was prominent in America at the time and figured there had to be a better way to lead people.

Greenleaf coined the term servant leadership in an essay in 1970:

The servant-leader is servant first. . . . It begins with the natural feeling that one wants to serve, to serve first. Then conscious choice brings one to aspire to lead. That person is sharply different from one who is leader first, perhaps because of the need to assuage an unusual power drive or to acquire material possessions. . . . The leader-first and the servant-first are two extreme types. Between them there are shadings and blends that are part of the infinite variety of human nature.

The difference manifests itself in the care taken by the servant-first to make sure that other people's highest priority needs are being served. The best test, and difficult to administer, is: Do those served grow as persons? Do they, while being served, become healthier, wiser, freer, more autonomous, more likely themselves to become servants? And, what is the effect on the least privileged in society? Will they benefit or at least not be further deprived?[86]

Larry Spears was the president and CEO of the Robert K. Greenleaf Center for Servant Leadership for seventeen years following Greenleaf's death in 1990. He spent two years studying Greenleaf's writings and formulated a list of the ten most frequently mentioned characteristics of an effective servant leader: listening, empathy, healing, awareness, persuasion, conceptualization, foresight, stewardship, commitment to the growth of people, and building community.[87]

Choose Service over Privilege

I challenge you to look across the landscape of American politics and find a single politician who employs a majority of those characteristics in their leadership style.

This crisis of servant leadership and sacrifice is evident in the obvious noise and confusion of the extremes as well as the lack of trust most Americans feel toward political—and even religious—institutions. The Middle's call to service and servant leadership is the first step in bringing America back from the radical extremes. The Middle is built on the foundation of service over personal gain—a sacrifice of what an individual can gain for the greater pursuit of what we can become. The Middle must revive this calling and a lifestyle of service, wherein the true gain is when we all move forward together.

The Middle knows we are a country lacking in servant leaders, even when we find the concept of servant leadership somewhat hard to define. We know it when we see it. There is no shortage of those claiming to be leaders through the demonization and "otherizing" of people. But the majority middle knows there is a need, if not a calling, for a revival of servant leadership if the extremes are going to lose their voice, allowing the Middle to regain its sense of national pride and purpose.

As previously stated in this book, America has become a nation of the zero-sum game. The days when leaders served for the good of others seem to be gone. More than fifty years ago, Greenleaf exalted the call of sacrifice for the good of others in his seminal work, *Servant Leadership*. His clarion call addressed a nation that seemed to be losing its soul: service that would be recognized as leadership. Now, "leadership" has become little more than a title—widely bestowed on people in power without evidence of greater good. Both sides of the political spectrum have chosen the path of power over service.

The call to serve is missing in so many areas of our lives—from CEOs in corporate America driving companies into bankruptcy and leaving with golden parachutes to ministers at mega churches getting rich from bombastic preaching and finger-pointing. Of course, our lack of service is nowhere more evident than in politics, where many elected officials come into office poor and leave quite wealthy.

Those in the Middle spend their days in service alongside people they agree with—and people they don't. Whether it's volunteering at schools, coaching youth sports, serving at a local church, or feeding the hungry—they do it without the expectation of a paycheck or recognition. They are simply doing what humanity does: serving without expecting anything in return.

The Middle wants the elected class to touch as little as possible, keep the country safe, help those in need, and stop interfering with everything. The Middle wants politicians to serve, and if they don't make the news, all the better. As I previously mentioned, in my time as mayor of Midland, Texas, I received a stipend of $75 a month. It wasn't about the money or recognition; it was a call to serve alongside city council members being paid $25 a month. This is what it used to mean to serve in elected office. The Middle is tired of the extremes gaming the system and selling votes for causes that pay them handsomely. The Middle wants to return to the kind of service that yields long-term good for everyone.

Choose Service over Privilege

One of my mayoral predecessors once told me that as mayor, "there is a good chance you will not see what you start come to completion." "So," he warned, "if you're looking for recognition, you are probably in the wrong position." This was a reminder that leadership is a long game, especially when it's truly servant leadership. Servant leadership isn't about looking for pats on the back, plaques, or parades; it prefers none of that even occur. Servant leadership is about leaving a legacy by building something better than what you inherited—for everyone, and not only those who agree with you.

The collapse of America's call to service has been a long time in the making, and it will take a while to turn this ship around. But the Middle is looking for leaders—Democrats, Republicans, or independents—willing to reject the game others have played for many years. The Middle wants men and women who can shift the tide to service over self. The extremes have so-called leaders seeking a platform, payday, and popularity; the Middle wants leaders who simply want to serve.

The Middle must demand this service of themselves in their neighborhoods, cities, and counties. The Middle must step into the roles of community service and volunteering, where we can make a real difference in the lives of our neighbors rather than being content to let the government step in to resolve every issue. The Middle would be well-served to remember what former President Ronald Reagan said: "We know from experience that the ten most frightening words in the English language are, 'I'm from the federal government, and I'm here to help.'"[88]

The Middle

The Middle might have to be the group that finally pushes for term limits for elected officials so their time to build a political dynasty is limited and so the arena remains open for those who want to serve for a season rather than making a living out of politics. When you consider that Nancy Pelosi, two-time Democratic Speaker of the House, has served in Congress for more than thirty-eight years, and Chuck Grassley, the Republican Senator from Iowa, has been in office in both the House of Representatives and Senate for more than half a century, it's no wonder so little ever gets done on Capitol Hill. The list of career politicians is long. Term limits would go a long way in weeding out corruption and preventing interest groups from influencing those in power for too long.

In the 1994 congressional elections, midway through President Bill Clinton's first term, Republicans called for term limits in Congress as part of its "Contract with America." This agenda captured unified control of Congress for the first time since 1952. Speaker of the House Newt Gingrich wrote, "We understand what our citizens know in their hearts: This is an America, standing on the doorstep of the twenty-first century, which no longer needs or desires a class of permanent career politicians who are there to solve each and every problem."[89] Gingrich argued that "a professional political class produces inertia" and that America would benefit from "continual waves of new leaders with fresh alternatives."[90]

Not surprisingly, the measure to impose twelve-year limits on both the House and Senate was soundly defeated in March 1995, with forty Republicans failing to support the measure, including thirty who had been in the House of Representatives for many years.

The Middle must demonstrate the reality that to whom much is given, much is required. We must change the perception that life in the United States is merely a right and instead demonstrate through acts and lives of service that being a citizen of this country is a call to serve one another.

Here are the marks of a new generation of servant leaders:

Empathy

In the words of educator and author Stephen Covey, "They see you."[91] True servant leaders are not just looking at you or using you. They know the reality of the struggles and troubles of life, and they want to find ways to help others succeed. People know the difference between flattery and empathy. The Middle has experienced the politics of flattery for decades, and they are searching for empathy. Far too much of what is perceived as empathy is mostly for political gain. Time and time again, they've heard politicians say, "I see you, and I won't forget you!" And time and time again, those same voters are forgotten the day after an election.

Listening

Americans want to hear their leaders speak with words that build rather than destroy our society. More importantly, they want their leaders to listen to the masses. Once again, Covey shared on this matter, saying, "We're filled with our rightness, our own autobiography. We want to be understood. Our conversations become collective monologues, and we never really understand what's going on inside another human being."[92]

The Middle has grown weary of the collective monologues of self-serving leadership and so-called experts. It longs for a return to a place of mutual respect and dedicated listening. It yearns for "knees-to-knees and eyeball-to-eyeball" listening, so our collective humanity improves.

Wisdom

America needs a perspective that goes beyond simply being "right." I have often told young leaders—and the occasional older leader—you can be wise, but you may not be right. Wisdom "sees more and before" others, and often even before the masses.

Wisdom protects us from the irrational impulses often inspired by crisis or uncertainty, while it becomes the steady lighthouse when storms pound the shoreline. Being "right" can often only be a product of current circumstances, while wisdom has the practiced perspective of experience and history.

Courage

True leaders display courage when they choose what's right over what's easy or popular, regardless of the cost. They're willing to make unpopular decisions and prioritize long-term benefits over short-term applause, even if it means upsetting their constituents, supporters, or members of their own political party. They're willing to face the music and stand alone against public opinion and media pressure.

We need more leaders like Margaret Chase Smith, the Republican senator from Maine, who famously defied McCarthyism when she delivered her "Declaration of Conscience" speech in the Senate Chamber on June 1, 1950, defending every American's "right to criticize . . . right to hold unpopular beliefs . . . right to protest."[93]

Humility

Only those leaders who truly understand their own strength know how to live and lead with humility. They have nothing to prove and are driven only by what others can gain. They listen to others, empower and serve others, admit their mistakes and learn from them, and willingly accept suggestions and criticism. They learn from others and give credit where it's due. They don't misuse their authority and prioritize supporting others.

Ulysses S. Grant, the commanding general of the Union Army during the American Civil War and eighteenth president of the United States, was one of the most humble leaders in our nation's history. Dismissed from the army during the Mexican-American War for his failures, Grant worked to improve himself as a leader of men. After the Union victory at the Battle of Vicksburg, Grant famously credited his soldiers, saying, "I have only given them direction."

Integrity

True leaders aren't going to sacrifice their principles—in public or in private—for individual gains or riches. They're honest, transparent, and keep their promises; they aren't afraid of the truth and don't blame others or make excuses for mistakes. Leaders with integrity are consistent in their beliefs and trustworthy, and they aren't afraid to intervene when they notice something going wrong. They walk the walk and stay true to their words and beliefs even in times of crisis.

Beyond "Honest Abe" Lincoln and George Washington—who allegedly could not tell a lie about chopping down a cherry tree—the late South African president and human rights activist Nelson Mandela is one of my favorite examples of a world leader with integrity. After fighting apartheid for much of his life, culminating in a prison sentence of twenty-seven years, Mandela became his country's first Black president in 1994. Instead of seeking revenge for those South Africans who had imprisoned him and upheld apartheid, Mandela focused on unification, forgiveness, and reconciliation. And, it should certainly be noted, Mandela served only one term before stepping down for the greater good of his country.

Sacrifice

Effective leaders are willing to prioritize the needs and well-being of others over their own personal ambitions and riches. These leaders will pay a personal price to allow their citizens or team members to move forward. In many ways, leadership is a service, and service comes with a cost.

The English author and inspirational speaker Simon Sinek put it this way:

> Our politicians fight to win, to keep themselves and their respective parties in power. They seem to spend more time working to consolidate power instead of sharing it

to get things done. Despite what they say, these are not the actions of those in service, those willing to sacrifice their personal ambitions for the greater good. Mandela, Dr. Martin Luther King Jr. and [Mahatma] Gandhi all went to jail instead of abandoning their beliefs. Our politicians seem more keen to abandon their beliefs to stay in office.[94]

Another former US president, Jimmy Carter, provided another excellent example of servant leadership. Many might argue that Carter had a far greater impact on the world after he left the White House, through his commitment to human rights, social justice, community service, global health, and peacekeeping.

After Carter died at the age of one hundred on December 29, 2024, *Houston Chronicle* columnist Chris Tomlinson recalled traveling with the former president to Rwanda in 1995. Carter was working to help end the bloody conflict between the Hutu government and Tutsi rebels, which had resulted in the genocide of more than one million people in one hundred days the year before. Even though Carter knew the odds of ending the civil war were low, he was at least going to try to stop it.

"These leaders know that I'm their last chance to rejoin the international community," Carter told Tomlinson. "If Jimmy Carter gives up on you, there's no one else coming."[95]

Whether it was helping build homes for low-income families through Habitat for Humanity into his nineties; founding the Carter Center in Atlanta to combat global disease, advance human rights, and promote peace around the world; or supporting racial and educational equality in the United States, Carter embodied doing what was right for the collective good. He consistently helped others without seeking recognition for his work.

Certainly, you don't have to be a world leader or politician to be a servant leader. I've come across many such individuals during my career in politics and pastoral ministry. Deborah Fikes, a member of the Council on Foreign Relations, who has been involved in peacemaking initiatives around the world, was the first person to take me to Sudan—a country which has been at war for much of the past seventy years. Two civil wars and separate conflicts in the Darfur region and South Sudan have left more than 2.5 million people dead and millions more displaced, orphaned, or widowed.

I was introduced to Bishop Elias Taban, founder of the Evangelical Presbyterian Church of Sudan and the nonprofit Water is Basic. Taban was a child solider until he escaped to Sudan in the first civil war (1955–1972). He later served as a colonel in the People's Liberation Army during the second civil war (1983–2005).

However, Bishop Taban's greatest work has been as an advocate for peace in his homeland. In 2012, he met with US Secretary of State Hillary Clinton to help resolve an oil dispute that threatened peace once again. Another man, Vernon Burger, was on the trip to Sudan with us. Vernon was only twenty-three years old when he founded His Voice Global to help orphans, vulnerable children, and widows in East Africa. Vernon and his wife, Amber, had been called to help those in need after taking separate trips to Africa. They met while working as interns at a church in Houston and were married in 2003.

With the help of a lot of good people in Midland, the Burgers opened their first orphanage in Sudan in 2005 and another one in 2008. Today, they're working in Kenya, South Sudan, Uganda, and North Korea.

During my trip to Sudan, my job was to brush orphans' teeth, and it was the first time many of them had seen a toothbrush. I still have visions of people dragging kids through the dirt to get them there; we had to close the orphanage's gates because we couldn't take any more. Those kids received a change of clothes and the first mattress they'd ever slept on. According to UNICEF, an estimated 52 million orphans in sub-Saharan Africa had lost one or both parents in 2019.[96]

At the end of our trip, Bishop Taban was driving us through the bush back to Uganda to get us to our airplane. We had to pass through various checkpoints, and Bishop Taban told us to look straight ahead and not to take photographs of the soldiers. Driving down these roads, I saw pieces of colorful fabric coming through the dirt. Bishop Taban told me it was the clothing of people who had been killed during the ongoing war. They'd built roads right over their bodies.

At one point during this trip, our truck broke down on a bush road. My friend and I were sitting on a log when a guy walked out of the brush carrying a machete and machine gun. I told my friend, "We're not going to get out of here."

We spent the night at a campground. As we were sitting around a campfire, I could hear rapid gunfire nearby. Bishop Taban told me that's how it was in Sudan. They'd also set entire fields on fire to drive out bush rats, which they would kill and eat. That's how hungry they were. After a long, treacherous journey, we finally made our way to Uganda. I sat on my hotel bed the next day and started weeping. After two weeks of backpacking through the bush, I was emotionally and physically drained. When we arrived at the airstrip, a friend of ours was standing in front of the plane, forcing the pilot to wait for us. There were geese, ducks, and goats in the cargo area with us. I looked outside, and one of the engine compartments was being held together by duct tape. I said a prayer and hoped for the best.

As we flew home, Bishop Taban was headed back to Sudan to save more orphans and widows. He could have left that war-torn area at any time, but he chose to remain there to help Sudan become a twenty-first-century nation with values and opportunities.

The world could use a lot more leaders like him.

CHAPTER 11

Conversation over Conflict

As the mayor of Midland, one of my most difficult tasks was handling the contentious debate of whether the name of Robert E. Lee High School should be changed in the aftermath of George Floyd's murder in 2020. Courtney Ratliff, a 1996 alumnus and former member of the marching band, launched the movement after attending a protest in Midland over police brutality around the country. Ratliff started an online petition to change the name of the high school and quickly secured more than ten thousand signatures. Of course, there were opposing petitions to continue honoring the Confederate general and not change the name, including one initiated by a county judge.

In the months after Floyd was killed by a police officer in Minneapolis, Minnesota, Confederate symbols and statues were being removed across the country, including a statue of Lee that represented Virginia in the National Statuary Collection in the US Capitol for more than a hundred years. In cities and towns around the country, streets, schools, and parks were being renamed, as America was reexamining its history of racism, division, and inequality. Robert E. Lee High Schools in Fairfax County, Virginia; Baton Rouge, Louisiana; Montgomery, Alabama; Jacksonville, Florida; and other towns and cities would eventually be renamed.

Many of the residents of Midland who opposed changing the name of our high school argued that the school's football success—three consecutive state titles in the late 1990s and early 2000s—would be lost. That might sound trivial—unless you're from Texas. I understood that Lee High had a proud and rich history. Among its graduates was former US First Lady Laura Bush, actor Tommy Lee Jones, NFL running back Cedric Benson, and US Army General Tommy Franks, who directed the attack on the Taliban in Afghanistan after the September 11, 2011, terrorist attacks and oversaw the 2003 invasion of Iraq and overthrow of dictator Saddam Hussein.

Others who didn't want to change the high school's name argued that the expense of rebranding the school at an estimated cost of $1 million wasn't prudent, especially at a time when the cost of a barrel of oil was dramatically down. The loudest opponents threatened to sue the district, recall school board members, or oppose a needed referendum to improve school facilities and address overcrowding.

I'm sharing this story with you because we've reached a tipping point in America when it comes to conversation and dialogue. Most of us can no longer talk to one another and work things out. Instead of listening and understanding the other side, our debates are little more than screaming and shouting, finger-pointing, and hurling accusations at the other side, whether they're true or not.

The Middle is built on a solid commitment to conversation, understanding, dialogue, and debate, wherein we return to the sage advice of author and educator Stephen Covey, who urged us to "seek first to understand before demanding to be understood."[97] The Middle has a duty to genuinely understand the viewpoints of those we disagree with to better engage in dialogue toward mutual ends rather than compete in a zero-sum game.

Most Americans have one goal when having a conversation with others, especially when it comes to politics or social issues: Make sure you get your point across. As the extremes continue to divide us, we've lost our willingness to listen to others intently and with compassion. We choose to ignore the other person who doesn't agree with us and pretend like we're listening, interrupt them mid-sentence, or cut them off—all to get our point across.

Not every conversation about politics must sound like a sports-talk radio debate about which team has the better quarterback—the New York Giants or Dallas Cowboys. You don't have to get in the last word. The Middle understands that not every conversation is about them. It acknowledges that our own life experiences and worldviews might not be the same as those of others.

As mayor, I listened intently to arguments from both sides when it came to the debate over renaming and rebranding Robert E. Lee High School. More than anything else, my Black friends and community leaders swayed me. Two of them were pastors, and the other was city councilman John Norman, whose brother, Josh, had been a football star at Lee High and the University of Oklahoma before going on to play in the NFL.

I took them to lunch and asked, "Okay, tell me what it's like to be Black in Midland."

African Americans made up only about 8 percent of the population. They told me stories of the past about being pulled over by police in town, and the cops already had their hands on their guns when they walked up to the car. These were not "anti-police" stories but simply real-life experiences most were not aware of. In all these conversations, I was struck by how meek and gentle my friends were in discussing their personal experiences. They held no animosity or grudge, and they were incredibly thankful for the question and the opportunity to discuss this matter. Again, when the rhetoric calms down and the listening begins, the easy answers of chosen sides subside, and new ways of thinking emerge.

When I decided to stand up for changing the name of Robert E. Lee High School, you would have thought I had become a card-carrying member of the Communist Party. In reality, I had simply had conversations with Black friends who were forced to play sports under the stars and bars of the Confederate battle flag and had to listen to the unmistakable melody of the Confederate anthem, "Dixie," being played by the marching band when the home team scored.

They had witnessed fans waving Confederate flags in the stands as they cheered on the Lee Rebels—yes, the school's mascot was a mustachioed Rebel wearing a cowboy hat. I could hear the pain in their voices during our discussions, and they experienced the same feelings when their children and grandchildren attended Robert E. Lee High.

In my research on the controversial subject, I became more and more convinced that much of the reasoning for the original naming and branding of Robert E. Lee High School was made in direct opposition to integration. The school had been founded in 1961 with the apparent purpose of sticking it to the federal government for forcing integration in Midland (when I moved there in 1999, the city was still working its way through mandatory busing of students, some forty-five years after the US Supreme Court's landmark *Brown v. Board of Education* decision, which ruled that separating children in public schools on the basis of race was unconstitutional).

For decades, Black students in Midland attended George Washington Carver High School, while white students enrolled at Midland High School. Carver High School won the city's first state title in football in 1961. When integration was forced on Midland following *Brown v. Board of Education*, city leaders decided to build a new school in the white section of town.

Texas Monthly, which has documented life in the Lone Star State since the seventies, wrote a story about the controversy in October 2020. The headline read, "'It's Going to Start a Civil War': A Midland School Discards Its Confederate Name." The article accurately explained why Robert E. Lee High School was built where it was built and why it was named what it was named:

In 1961, the district opened a new high school on the northwest side of town, just about as far away as one could get from the city's predominantly minority neighborhoods. Thanks to redlining and the economic segregation of neighborhoods, the new school was almost certain to be entirely white. Should the district's intentions be unclear, the school board named the campus Robert E. Lee High School and chose a mascot that perfectly captured the community's prevailing "here's-where-you-can-shove-it" attitude toward outside authority: the Rebels.[98]

When I talked to people who opposed changing the name of the high school, one of their most cited reasons was that they didn't want to lose their high school memories. What that meant to me was that they hadn't done their research. I had served as the football team's chaplain and worked as the radio play-by-play announcer, so I was well aware of how important "Friday Night Lights" was to so many in the city.

The entire controversy was a lesson for me in what it means to empathetically listen and form a new question. By listening to others and doing my own research, I arrived at a new question. It was not whether we should rename the school. Instead, the question was, "If we opened a new school today, in 2020, would we name it after Robert E. Lee, sing 'Dixie,' and fly the Rebel flag of the South?"

Absolutely not.

I arrived at this new question only by listening deeply to my Black friends who presented me with a new perspective and question with gracious hearts and kind words. I decided to write an op-ed in the *Midland Reporter-Telegram* in August 2020 and took a chance by presenting the city my new question. The number of negative emails I'd received already outweighed the positive ones by about ten to one, so I was prepared for whatever was coming next.

In the op-ed, I attempted to explain my reasoning for supporting a name change and rebranding:

> I served as the chaplain for the Lee Rebels football team, watched all my kids wear the maroon, silver and white and compete in extracurricular activities, and yes, I even got kicked out of a game for yelling at the ref (a memory not worth keeping!). Nevertheless, memories, attachments and accomplishments are not what is at stake in the change we are discussing. I would suggest that doing what is right is what is at stake in this moment of our time.[99]

I attempted to explain to Midland's residents that if the city had needed a new high school in 2019, there wasn't any way it would have been named after Lee, a Confederate general who supported a person's right to own slaves. We were no longer living in the fifties and sixties, when many Americans opposed desegregating schools. Up until the late 1960s in Midland, home deeds included the following provision: "No premises or lots or parts thereof shall ever be used or conveyed to any person of any race or descent other than persons of the Caucasian race." We were no longer living in those forgettable times.

The op-ed continued:

> By the 21st century most of us would have had meaningful and honest conversations with our Black friends in an effort to understand what the exaltation of the "South" and the memory of Dixie actually felt like to them. They would tell us stories of fathers and grandfathers who had to search out places they could live, segregated schools to attend and water fountains to drink from; we would then begin to feel a little of what it might feel like to celebrate the "Rebel Spirit" and the Lee heritage and history rooted in a past dedicated to limited access to life, liberty and the pursuit of happiness.[100]

Changing the name of a high school because it brought pain to a segment of our population was not about erasing history, memories, or pride, nor was it about bowing to the so-called cancel culture. As I wrote back then, it was about realizing that the right action of today should have been the right action of yesterday, and that this was the day we got to do it over for the right reasons.

After that lunch meeting with my Black friends who were leaders in Midland, I did my own homework on Robert E. Lee High School. There were many things that my personal research revealed that don't need to be repeated. In the end, I decided that the deeply personal stories they shared with me went much deeper than someone's memories of state titles or prom nights. In fact, most of the people who spoke to me about changing the name of Lee High never expressed concern for the legitimacy of the feelings and life experiences of my Black friends.

Through the controversy, there was very little effort by many to understand the perspective of another who might view history, names, and titles dramatically differently than they do. While there were many white residents of Midland who believed it was time for a name change, the volume of emails I received indicated a perception that I was ruining the city's history by advocating that the school board change the name of the high school.

In the end, the Midland Independent School District board voted six to one to change the name. It was rebranded as Legacy High School. The school's mascot remained the Rebels, although the Confederate general was replaced with an American Revolutionary War soldier. In August 2025, the Midland Independent School District's board of trustees voted to change the name back to Robert E. Lee High School, calling previous name changes and the removal of statues as an attack on the "country's heritage."[101]

This nation has been marked by sharp disagreements since the days of its founding, through various administrations and seasons of history. The defining difference between then and now is the display of mature civility marked by mutual respect that has been lost in the quest for power on the extremes of both sides. The Middle understands how to listen intently, with empathy and understanding.

No one disagrees that partisanship and vigorous debate have taken place from our founding. Even a few of the Founding Fathers had some choice words for one another. But the majority practice of civility seemed to prevail more often than not. Time and lengthy discussion, a slow press, and slow-traveling news allowed tempers to moderate and debate to ensue.

Today, there is little to no space for breathing between posts and reposts on social media, let alone much time for serious meditations and consequent dialogue. This scourge of instant attacks of one another—this back-and-forth vitriol across America—calls for a new generation of leaders who will resist the urge to post whatever comes to mind without having a real conversation with those they're attacking.

Throughout my civic and professional life, I've tried to follow the lead of my late friend, Michael Trost, who served on the Midland City Council for three terms. Michael was a bit of a contrarian, and he and I did not always see eye to eye on certain issues, but he was a throwback gentleman. There were times when he'd call me at home at night to discuss our differing views, or we'd have a beer together to hash out our disagreements privately. He never once threw someone else under the bus in public and showed others great respect—even when he didn't agree with them. He honored conversation over conflict in many ways.

Conversely, our country has turned a corner down a dangerous path, in which we seem to honor those who can be the loudest and angriest in conflict and condemnation. This is not servant or effective leadership, and frankly, it's the behavior and modus operandi of the weak and abusive. We must return to a time of honoring one another with humility and meekness. If we are going to push back against abusive extremes, we must be willing to practice and honor conversation over conflict.

When I was pastoring, I had the opportunity to train a number of young preachers. I spent much time teaching them how to prepare and deliver a sermon. I found that my most beneficial teaching moments came after an aspiring preacher gave a sermon and we sat together to review his or her content, delivery, and performance. Oftentimes, young preachers have wonderful material and eloquent delivery in their sermons, but they fail to connect with their congregation for whatever reason. In most instances, this lack of connection did not come from inadequate content or answers. More times than not, it came from these young pastors lacking real-life experience.

Anyone can preach about trust and principles from the Bible's instruction regarding marriage and raising children. But without actual life experiences of building a family, you're not going to have any idea about what it's like to be married or raise children. In other words, it goes back to having the right answers but missing the question, and one of my favorite sayings, "You might be right, but you are not wise."

Today, many people mistakenly view their observations and opinions as facts, even when they lack historical perspective or a full understanding of life experience. Unfortunately, we live in a time when many people believe that simply having a screen name or handle on social media makes them an expert on issues they know very little about. Their quest for likes, clicks, and page views causes them to ignore how others are feeling in reaction to their opinions and posts.

The Middle is painfully aware that the extremes are shouting in echo chambers fueled by this perceived popularity. The majority middle longs for listening. It longs for the self-proclaimed "experts" to stop talking and take time to listen.

The Middle is ready to tackle this challenge in daily life and demonstrate to others how to embrace conversation over conflict, and what it means to listen and seek understanding before turning up the volume.

CHAPTER 12

Humble History

In the buildup to the 2024 United States presidential election, politicians on both sides of the aisle were calling it the "most important election" in American history. Did anyone stop to think about the very first presidential election of our nation? Surely, the election of Abraham Lincoln—who abolished slavery and reunited a fractured nation—stands as a moment of greater consequence, as do Franklin D. Roosevelt's unprecedented wartime victories. Or perhaps the historic ascent of John F. Kennedy, the first non-Protestant president, marked a more profound turning point?

While people on the extreme edges have a penchant for hyperbole when it comes to the current political landscape and what's at stake in America, those in the Middle remind themselves that history is constantly being written and refined, and, more importantly, that everyone is a part of the fabric of the long thread of the story.

The Middle

As Americans, we must have humility to understand that thousands of years came before us, and there will most likely be thousands more to follow. We are not the be-all and end-all of the global and cosmic story. We would be well-served to study ancient kingdoms and how they often fell from the hubris of their inflated opinion of themselves—the arrogance built on a one-sided, extreme view that excluded others.

Look no further than the ancient Roman Empire. Rome was ruled under a republic for more than five hundred years, and the Romans inspired our Founding Fathers to enact separation of powers, checks and balances, and presidential veto. While hubris has often been cited as the primary reason for the fall of the Roman Empire, other historians argue that complacency was more likely the cause. Rome's rulers became detached from the needs of their people, resulting in a sizable wealth gap and multiyear cycles of legislative gridlock that led to an uprising.

Sound familiar?

"Taking the strength of their republic for granted, they never let republican principles dissuade them from a potent line of attack against a political opponent," wrote Edward J. Watts, history professor at the University of California, Davis. "This shortsightedness normalized a form of political combat in which the Republic no longer set the rules and no longer protected the losers. Robbed of its institutional defenses, the Republic could not prevent Rome's descent into civil war or stop the emergence of a Roman autocracy. And Romans were shocked when the Republic's impotence was finally revealed."[102]

Humble History

Watts, the author of *Mortal Republic: How Rome Fell into Tyranny*, saw many of the same problems in America today. He argued that our country has "turned a blind eye to the damage that the past generation of political dysfunction has done to our republic."[103]

"Morally and legally dubious political tactics often seemed relatively harmless when they benefited people and policies that one approved," Watts wrote. "But today Americans who continue to vote for the senators who block judicial nominations made by the opposing party, representatives who endorse government shutdowns, and presidents who traffic in threats and intimidation should realize that these decisions weaken our republic. We can avoid the complacency that doomed the Roman Republic. If we do not, there is a real risk that Americans will repeat Rome's mistake."[104]

Our Founding Fathers and early leaders knew the success of our republic depended on finding solutions that allowed the government to stay out of people's lives as much as possible, leaving them to pursue their dreams. However, in the insatiable desire for power, driven by ever-increasing special interests on both sides of the political and religious edges, the Middle has been caught in the crossfire of this power grab. The Middle is tired of the irrational arrogance of the extremes and realizes that neither represents the common pursuit of living free.

There was a man I had the privilege of knowing while serving as a pastor in Midland. His name was Brad, and he was a giant of a man. Our church experienced rapid growth through the years and substantial respect in the community. In my role, I became more and more involved in local and state matters. Brad and I met often for lunch at a local Mexican restaurant, where we had great conversations about myriad life issues. Without fail, as we exchanged our farewells in the parking lot after our meetings, Brad would tell me, "Don't forget where you came from!"

Brad's comment influenced me more than one might expect—maybe because it reminded me of my humble beginnings, both as a child and an adult, which could have been easily forgotten with the success and notoriety we were experiencing.

Whatever the reason, I have a habit of often mentally reminding myself to never forget where I started. Whether exiting the Oval Office in the White House, shaking the hands of past US presidents, attending meetings at the United Nations, or sitting across the table from a homeless person, my mental message is the same: *Never forget where you came from*. As a nation, we would be wise to heed this admonition and never forget where we came from.

In one form or another, we have been warned that those who ignore history are doomed to repeat it. It takes humility to pause and reflect on the words of Solomon in the Bible:

> What has been is what will be, and what has been done is what will be done, and there is nothing new under the sun. Is there a thing of which it is said, "See, this is new"? It has been already in the ages before us. There is no remembrance of former things, nor will there be any remembrance of later things yet to be among those who come after. (Ecclesiastes 1:9–11)

Humble History

Of course, the easy response to Solomon's advice is, "That's crazy! Nobody had an iPhone thirty years ago! Sure, there is something new under the sun." However, this lazy assertion about technology misses the point. Sure, technology advances, but the core matters of life—relationships—never change. Whether national, international, local, or at home, what's not new is the dynamic of what makes life worthwhile or deadly—relationships and how we treat one another.

We would be wise to humbly remember the events in American history that nearly destroyed us:

- The founding of our country started with the thirteen colonies' collective decision to break away from the British government, which had wrongly taxed the colonists to pay for the monarchy's huge debts from the French and Indian War (1754–1763). Colonists argued they shouldn't be taxed without having representatives in the British Parliament. Following the Tax Act, Townshend Act, and Tea Act, which placed taxes on colonists for legal documents, newspapers, and other essential goods such as tea, glass, and paper, colonists began to realize that independence was the only solution. Would they have fought against tyranny and rallied together in the name of liberty if they hadn't realized their cause was greater than any one person?

- The main cause of the American Civil War (1861–1865) was slavery, but there were also deeper political, economic, and cultural divisions that had been building for decades in our nation. Northern states were becoming more industrialized and opposed slavery expanding into Western territories. The Southern economy depended on slave labor, and the election of Lincoln and the Republican Party, which opposed slavery, threatened the South's way of life. The Northern states wanted a strong federal government that could control the expansion of slavery, while Southerners argued that states had the right to govern themselves.

During the growing crisis between North and South, our nation lost its moral compass—and with it, the humility to listen, learn, and see one another as fellow human beings. The polarized extremes—whether in the name of abolition or the defense of the Southern way of life—led many to forget the foundational truth that "all men are created equal, and endowed by their Creator with certain unalienable rights." Instead, pride, greed, and a refusal to understand one another fueled the descent into the deadliest conflict in American history. By the war's end, an estimated 750,000 Union and Confederate soldiers had lost their lives. Indeed, pride comes before the fall.

- Most Americans wanted to stay out of foreign wars in the early twentieth century. However, unrestricted submarine warfare by Germany and the Zimmerman Telegram pushed the United States toward involvement in World War I, which was largely a European conflict. Then, less than three decades later, the rise of Adolf Hitler and Nazi

Germany eventually forced a reckoning in America to stop fascism. The technology of war changed everything, while hubris, pride, and even unhinged racism led people away from one another rather than toward one another in humility, gentleness, and meekness to understand differences and come to solutions of historical affect. Instead, while technology advanced and the power of humanity to control its environment progressed, bitterness and hatred drove people and nations further and further apart and into the extremes. Sadly, they eventually decided the only way to resolve it was to kill one another and drop atomic bombs on Hiroshima and Nagasaki in Japan to end World War II.

- Nearly two centuries after the founding of the United States, we were setting a course for the Moon, driving cars, and flying around the world in the 1950s and 1960s. Sadly, at the same time, many Americans still could not vote, drink from water fountains, or even live in certain neighborhoods because of the color of their skin. Civil rights leaders, including Martin Luther King Jr., John F. Kennedy, Malcolm X, and others, fell victim to assassins' bullets. Bloody battles between segregationists and everyday citizens took place on bridges and roads across the South. Those who wanted to rally for civil rights were turned away, as a lack of humility, gentleness, and meekness drove Americans into the extremes. Too many died during this long fight, and our country's leadership was forced into the passage of humility that recognized we either believed all men were created equal and acted like it—or we did not.

Partisanship is not new, and neither is the conviction that we live in a world of binary right and wrong. But even in the debates about who or what is right or wrong, we must still come to grips with a reality that we can either *live with and for* one another through our issues or *go through* one another with our issues—regardless of the cost.

If America is going to advance beyond these issues, it will require a new generation of humble and strong leaders to hold tight to their convictions of black and white and right and wrong. It will take a renewed effort to not let the extremes turn conviction of right and wrong into destruction of one another, either by words or by force.

As I get older, I have often shared with young leaders looking for guidance that the list of convictions worth "building a bridge to die on" grows shorter with age. I have also reminded them that one conviction remains true: Every person is created by God and deserves respect and honor. We may disagree on certain issues, but we do not have the right to be disrespectful. As we know from our history, the path of disrespect allows the extremes to capitalize on dishonor that drives petty partisanship into full-blown hatred that can destroy us. We would be wise to humbly reflect on the dangers of our human nature, as revealed throughout history.

Humble History

In these moments, we would do well to remember the cautionary stories written by those before us. As Saint Francis wisely instructed, "Seek rather to comfort than to be comforted, to understand rather than to be understood."[105] I would add seek with humility, and with an eye on the past, because remembering where we've been can keep us grounded in where we need to go.

More than anything else, remember that pride comes before the fall.

If it hasn't been obvious before now, I'll say it loud and clear: I love football. I love the rivalries, pageantry, and camaraderie that come with the sport, especially college football. One of my favorite films is *Remember the Titans*, in which Denzel Washington plays Herman Boone, a Black football coach hired by T. C. Williams High School in Alexandria, Virginia, to help integrate what was previously an all-white school in the early 1970s.

As Boone is leading his players—both Black and white—on an early morning training run during preseason camp, he stops at the edge of a graveyard. It was the edge of the site where the Battle of Gettysburg took place in and around Gettysburg, Pennsylvania, during the American Civil War. The three-day battle between the Union and Confederate armies—July 1 to July 3, 1863—was the deadliest single conflict in the war and became a turning point, with the Union Army turning away General Robert E. Lee's second quest to invade the North.

"Anybody know what this place is?" Washington asks his players in *Remember the Titans*. "This is Gettysburg. This is where they fought the Battle of Gettysburg. Fifty thousand men died right here on this field, fightin' the same fight that we're still fightin' amongst ourselves today. This green field right here was painted red, bubblin' with the blood of young boys, smoke and hot lead pourin' right through their bodies. Listen to their souls, men: 'I killed my brother with malice in my heart. Hatred destroyed my family.' You listen. And you take a lesson from the dead."[106]

Whether there is some Hollywood license in Coach Boone's speech is beside the point. The words, lessons, and sentiment ring true, even today. We must be willing to take a hard, honest, and humble look at our past so we don't repeat the mistakes that, at times, led America to great tragedy.

Voices of the past will speak volumes to us if we'll only listen. The voices of our humble past teach us that life is short and that when it's all over, we'll take nothing with us to the grave except how we treated others and how they remember us treating them. No matter what we've done or accomplished in life, most people will only remember if we were decent and whether we enhanced the lives of others or not.

Years ago, I was asked to officiate the funeral of a man I hadn't known personally. As I met with his family to learn more about their father and husband, I asked each of them to share their memories and stories about him. One by one, I went around the room. Much to my surprise, each of his family members responded, "I cannot think of any." I sat dumbfounded, thinking this couldn't possibly be true, so I asked them again. To my sadness, their answers remained the same.

This is a tragic story and a painful reminder that, if we are not

Humble History

careful, those who follow us in a rush to the cliff of extremism will have the same things to say about us and what we did. They will not remember the good things we said about one another and the work we did together and for one another. Instead, they will mourn that we forsook our higher ideals to prove our narrow point. They will be left with a poor example of what it means to love and honor one another, and instead be left with the cynicism of extremism rather than the promise of one nation under God and indivisible. Sometimes the little reminders of small funerals can serve as a large reminder of the bigger issues we must deal with.

In the spirit of Gettysburg, we might do well to humbly reflect on the historic words of Lincoln at the dedication of the Soldiers' National Cemetery in Gettysburg, only a few months after the bloody battle that killed so many sons and fathers:

> Four score and seven years ago our fathers brought forth on this continent, a new nation, conceived in Liberty, and dedicated to the proposition that all men are created equal. Now we are engaged in a great civil war, testing whether that nation, or any nation so conceived and so dedicated, can long endure. We are met on a great battlefield of that war. We have come to dedicate a portion of that field, as a final resting place for those who here gave their lives that that nation might live. It is altogether fitting and proper that we should do this.
>
> But, in a larger sense, we can not dedicate—we can not consecrate—we can not hallow—this ground.

The brave men, living and dead, who struggled here, have consecrated it, far above our poor power to add or detract. The world will little note, nor long remember what we say here, but it can never forget what they did here. It is for us the living, rather, to be dedicated here to the unfinished work which they who fought here have thus far so nobly advanced.

It is rather for us to be here dedicated to the great task remaining before us—that from these honored dead we take increased devotion to that cause for which they gave the last full measure of devotion—that we here highly resolve that these dead shall not have died in vain—that this nation, under God, shall have a new birth of freedom—and that government of the people, by the people, for the people, shall not perish from the earth.[107]

As Lincoln noted at the end of his two-minute speech, "Read these words carefully and reflect on them deeply."[108]

CHAPTER 13

Curious Rather Than Right

O n April 13, 1970, people in America and around the world were glued to their TVs as NASA engineers worked tirelessly to bring the Apollo 13 crew back to Earth after an oxygen tank exploded in the service module, leaving the spacecraft inoperable.

NASA abandoned its plans to send the Apollo 13 crew to the Moon and turned its energy to safely returning Commander Jim Lovell, Command Module Pilot Jack Swigert, and Lunar Module Pilot Fred Haise. Because the command module, Odyssey, had lost power and oxygen, the crew had to move to the smaller lunar module, Aquarius, which was still operable. There was one very significant problem: Aquarius had been designed for only two astronauts, so there wasn't enough oxygen and life support for all three of them.

After Swigert's now-famous line, "Houston, we've had a problem,"[109] reached Mission Control at Johnson Space Center in

The Middle

Houston, Texas, NASA engineers and support teams sprang into action, working tirelessly to save the astronauts and bring them home safely. While Apollo 13 flight director Gene Kranz is often attributed with saying, "Failure is not an option," he never actually said it (actor Ed Harris did say it in the 1995 film about the failed space mission). Kranz later noted in his autobiography that "Failure is not an option" was Mission Control's creed.[110]

Through incredible collaboration, NASA engineers on the ground invented solutions in real time, such as using duct tape, plastic bags, cardboard, and socks to construct additional carbon dioxide filters. Mathematicians used simulators and slide rules to calculate manual burns for course corrections and manually aligning the spacecraft for reentry. Even the most die-hard skeptic had to set aside his or her doubts and convictions of impossibility and work toward a solution.

In one of America's greatest moments, the Apollo 13 crew made a dramatic and frigid journey around the Moon before safely splashing down in the Pacific Ocean on April 17, 1970.

In many ways, I might argue that the challenges we face in America today are every bit as serious as getting men back from outer space on a broken spaceship. If we don't figure out a way to come together to work toward the common good, we may not die from carbon dioxide poisoning or orbital reentry, but we'll seemingly be spinning in space if the extremes convince us one side is right and the other side is wrong. The extremes want us to believe that we have nothing to learn from each other—and that the other side doesn't deserve to live within the promise of life, liberty, and happiness.

One of my favorite anecdotes involving President Abraham Lincoln is his relationship with Edwin Stanton, who had long been Lincoln's legal rival and a steadfast opponent of the president and the Republican Party. However, when Lincoln needed a capable Secretary of War at the height of the American Civil War, he turned to Stanton, who had once called him the "original gorilla."

The story goes that a congressman who was hoping to curry favor with the president told Lincoln that Stanton had called him a "damned fool" for supporting another lawmaker's pet project. When told of Stanton's insult, Lincoln calmly responded, "If Stanton said I was a damned fool, then I must be one, for he is nearly always right and generally says what he means. I will step over and see him."[111]

The Middle is built on a willingness to doubt our certainty and to listen to others' concerns about our position. The most dangerous person is the fanatic who has chosen to believe they have nothing more to learn within their belief system, and thereby considers their view to be the only truth. The extremes of the left and right must be met with an equally aggressive commitment to constant learning and adjustment, wherein our personal understanding of truth is often refined but rarely 100 percent certain.

The ancient Greek philosopher Socrates might have said it best—or at least it has been attributed to him for centuries: "All I know is that I know nothing." While Socrates is still regarded as one of the great thinkers and founders of Western philosophy, he had a clear understanding that there are limits to knowledge and the human mind. He was also open to new ideas and believed that we should question things in life and not take widely accepted beliefs as gospel.

This doesn't mean there is no such thing as absolute truth. There are things I believe with all my heart. But my deep belief system still cannot prohibit me from listening to another point of view and respecting the person holding that view.

In an attempt to trap Jesus in a test about the absolute law, the religious elite of His day asked Him what the greatest commandment was. Those questioning Him were certain of their "rightness" and were ready to pounce when He answered. The answer Jesus gave was simple and to the point: The greatest commandments were to love God and love others. This was not an excuse to avoid right and wrong.

First Corinthians 13, a popular passage often read aloud in weddings, declares,

> Love is patient and kind; love does not envy or boast; it is not arrogant or rude. It does not insist on its own way; it is not irritable or resentful; it does not rejoice at wrongdoing, but rejoices with the truth. Love bears all things, believes all things, hopes all things, endures all things. Love never ends. . . . So now faith, hope, and love abide, these three; but the greatest of these is love. (1 Corinthians 13:4–8, 13)

That last line really lowers the boom: faith, hope, and love are all important, but the greatest of these qualities is love. In other words, we can still hold on to our beliefs and convictions, but we must do so with the curiosity rooted in a practice of love that wants to serve others rather than prove them wrong or humiliate them. I can still be right, but I can do it with honor. I can also find out, through curiosity, that I am wrong and have the opportunity to change my mind.

Some people must always be right, and they can't stand to lose an argument, even when there's compelling evidence to prove them wrong. They seek out information that supports their beliefs—even if it's rejected widely as "fake news"—and discount data that contradicts them. In recent years, political scientists have called this phenomenon *confirmation bias*.

Liberals tend to believe everything they hear on CNN but insist everything on Fox News is strongly biased or inaccurate. Conversely, conservatives believe CNN is a propaganda machine for liberals, while Fox News and Newsmax TV are bastions of sound journalism.

While serving as mayor, I often told my friends and family, "I don't care where you get your news; you need to assume you are only getting about 25 percent of the story." In an era when opinion masquerading as fact is constantly bombarding us, we must cultivate a mindset of curiosity if we are ever going to hear and respect one another. But sadly, that's not where we are today in America. A Pew Research Center study noted that 70 percent of self-described liberal Democrats and 16 percent of conservative Republicans trusted CNN—an astounding 54-percent gap between parties. However, 75 percent of conservative Republicans and 12 percent of liberal Democrats trusted Fox News—an even wider gap of 63 percentage points.[112]

The Middle

During a speech at Cornell College in Iowa on October 15, 1962, Dr. Martin Luther King Jr., famously said, "I am convinced that men hate each other because they fear each other. They fear each other because they don't know each other, and they don't know each other because they don't communicate with each other, and they don't communicate with each other because they are separated from each other."[113] The Middle is committed to ending the separation, communicating with the other side, and remaining curious rather than right.

One of my favorite Netflix shows of the past few years is *Ted Lasso*, in which the main character, portrayed by actor Jason Sudeikis, is an American college football coach who is hired to coach an English soccer team. The female owner of the AFC Richmond team, Rebecca Welton, wants her handpicked coach with no experience in soccer to fail. Her unfaithful ex-husband, Rupert, loves the team more than anything else, and Rebecca, blinded by heartbreak, sets out to destroy the thing he loved most.

In one of the best scenes, Ted and Rebecca run into Rupert and his younger fiancée in a pub. After Rupert informs Rebecca that he plans to attend every AFC Richmond game with his new trophy wife, Ted challenges Rupert to a game of darts. They wager on the outcome: If Rupert wins, he gets to choose the team's starting lineup for two games; if Ted comes out on top, Rupert has to stay away from the owners' box. Everyone in the pub thinks Ted is crazy because Rupert is such an accomplished player.

As Rupert pulls out his custom darts, Ted haphazardly throws darts like he's never played the game before. The critical moment comes when Ted falls behind and has to make a comeback to win the match. As he makes a series of throws to win, Ted tells the story of how he had, in fact, played a lot of darts in a sports bar with his dad while growing up. He shared that he'd been overlooked throughout his life and had never understood why—until he saw a quote from the poet Walt Whitman painted on a wall at his son's school: "Be curious, not judgmental."

"So I get back in my car and I'm driving to work, and all of a sudden it hits me," Ted tells Rupert. "All them fellas that used to belittle me, not a single one of them were curious. They thought they had everything all figured out, so they judged everything, and they judged everyone. And I realized their underestimating me . . . who I was had nothing to do with it. 'Cause if they were curious, they would have asked questions. You know?"[114]

Just as Ted prepares to throw a final bull's-eye, he tells Rupert, "Questions like, 'Have you played a lot of darts, Ted?'"[115]

Being curious and asking questions is a lost practice we must return to if we are going to regain the Middle. As you go through life, be curious about what others think and why they think it. Be curious about the story behind a person's life—you've never walked in their shoes. Be curious as to why someone believes what he or she believes, and as to why someone might disagree with you.

We are indeed a unique and varied people, with all kinds of stories, backgrounds, hurts, and hang-ups. We would be wise to be more like Ted Lasso and choose to be curious rather than certain. Embrace curiosity over judgment. Approach conversations with an open mind, focusing on what others contribute to the discussion, rather than solely on what we bring.

As I've mentioned in prior chapters, you can be right and still not be wise. Wisdom is not being smart but having a broad and proper perspective. We have become a nation with narrow perspectives, wound up in small, individual stories. We fail to grasp the larger perspective of a collective melting pot of people. We need to seek first to understand one another before leveling accusations and judgments.

It takes great maturity and intestinal fortitude to put one's opinions and convictions on the table and enter into a discussion rooted in curiosity. Over the past several years, it has become too commonplace for people to assume that within our narrow view of the world—emboldened by algorithmic social media—we have all the answers and only our perspective is correct.

The reality is that the world and our nation are too diverse and nuanced for any one of us to stake our unchallenged claims on truth. Yet we're told we're correct over and over again because we separate ourselves from others into tribes of extremes and surround ourselves with teams of "yes people." At some point, we must each choose to be more curious than certain. More than anything else, remember that one's personal foundation does not have to be compromised in order to listen and perhaps find another way to solve a collective problem.

It is to this third way that we must turn, finding a way to push off from the shores of the safe extremes and get into a river of discovery and a life together, if each and every one of us is going to find the American dream.

If we are ever to return to respecting our common humanity and find a path forward together, we must commit to being *curious* as much as, if not more than, being *right*. We must foster an attitude and practice of curiosity.

Humility is a word used often, but it's not a common practice in much of our society today. As an old friend used to say, "Humility is the choice to stop thinking so highly of yourself and choosing to think more highly of others." Humility is the personal practice of truly believing you have more to learn and of being willing to learn more from others. Humility takes to heart the idea that you still have much to learn and can learn from others you might even disagree with.

It's becoming increasingly difficult to find examples of public humility among so-called leaders of our day. From presidents to preachers to politicians, we mostly hear about how great they are, what they've done for us, and how bad the other side is. Rarely do we hear or see examples of humility that reach across aisles of disagreement to find a third way. It seems everywhere we turn, someone is trying to take credit for an accomplishment while discrediting the other side. The majority middle in our nation is worn out with experts. The experts among us spend all their time arguing with the other experts, and we don't seem to be any better off, as the people in charge dig in their heels on seemingly every important issue while failing to be curious.

The Middle is not a place where one side always loses and the other wins—like the extremes. It is a place where we humbly approach one another with a desire to learn. We don't begin by trying to prove the other wrong, but instead with a curiosity that recognizes we can all learn from one another.

CHAPTER 14

Our Way over My Way

One of the most fulfilling experiences of my professional life was being appointed to the inaugural class of the Presidential Leadership Scholars program in 2015. It was one of the most consequential moments in my life, as I truly realized that humanity is a collection of differing backgrounds, beliefs, and life experiences far more diverse than I had ever imagined.

The presidential centers of Lyndon B. Johnson, George H. W. Bush, William J. Clinton, and George W. Bush collaborated to create the six-month program that brought sixty scholars together to learn from past presidents, administration officials, and academics from around the world. It was a wonderful opportunity to learn from some of the smartest people in our country and to network with folks from all walks of life. The program focused on vision and communications, decision-making, influence and persuasion, and coalition building.

While it was a life-altering experience, I'll never forget an interaction at one of our first meetings together at George Washington's Mount Vernon in Virginia. I was talking to a conservationist from Colorado. Once I informed him that I was from Midland, Texas, home of many of the largest oil and gas producers in the world, the conservationist flippantly asked, "Why do you guys like killing polar bears?"

I was stunned and wasn't sure how to respond. I couldn't believe that's how he chose to start a conversation with someone he'd never met.

"They make really good rugs," I joked to him.

Once the conservationist picked his jaw up from the floor, I said, "Maybe we can restart this conversation and get to know each other. Then we can talk about conservation, oil and gas, global warming, and all the other things that seem to divide us." Rather than taking the extreme bait like a trout consuming a caddis fly in a mountain stream, I chose to ask him a few questions instead. I decided to be curious so he could get to know me, and so I could get to know him.

Believe it or not, we ended up having a very pleasant and productive conversation that day. We got to know each other decently well over the course of the Presidential Leadership Scholars program. We addressed other important matters, finding common ground and solutions that worked for both parties. I know I learned quite a bit from him, and I'm hoping he learned a little bit from me too. I'm certain we learned more from each other than we could have learned on our own.

Our Way over My Way

Back in 1992, the book that changed my life outside of the Bible was Stephen Covey's *Seven Habits of Highly Effective People*. It was a true game changer for my life. Covey's fourth habit says, "Think Win/Win," and the fifth is, "Seek First to Understand, Then to Be Understood."[116]

I remember reading Covey's idea of synergy for the first time as a twenty-two-year-old. I wasn't quite sure how to apply it to my life at the time, but deep in my soul, I knew the inherent truth in seeing and hearing one another and seeking a better path together than we could travel alone. It took me a couple of decades to fully appreciate the value of synergy, but now, later in life, I am convinced that Covey was speaking as a prophet with a message we would all need to hear in a time he only glimpsed.

Over four decades ago, Covey wrote,

> Valuing our differences is the essence of synergy—the mental, the emotional, the psychological differences between people. And the key to valuing those differences is to realize that all people see the world, not as it is, but as they are. Many people have not really experienced even a moderate degree of synergy in their family life or . . . other interactions. They've been trained and scripted into defensive and protective communications or into believing that life or other people can't be trusted. . . . Synergy is almost as if a group collectively agrees to subordinate old scripts and to write new a one.[117]

The Middle

I was raised in a world of the seventies and eighties that demanded treating others with respect and being curious before demanding to be understood. Now, as a retired pastor and politician, I sadly realize that no one is trying to understand where the other person is coming from. There are no conversations taking place before opinions and assumptions are made. We're too quick to label others as being either for or against us without fully understanding who they are.

The Middle is committed to the pursuit of the third way of synergy—and not just win-lose scenarios. A great nation is built on great thinkers coming together to discover the power of synergistic thinking over and against either-or beliefs. It requires brave and humble people and leaders to seek the *best* answer together rather than a *good* answer alone. The third way isn't a lukewarm compromise; it's a radically different approach that reshapes the problem to prioritize shared solutions over one-sided victories. It's about finding the middle ground so we can all benefit from solving a problem.

America cannot get to a third way—a better way—until both dominant political parties realize they have something to learn from each other. Only when they accept that they can learn something from the other side and are willing to listen to differing views will they come up with a better solution for all of us. Leaders on both sides of the aisle must adopt a third way of thinking—one rooted in a shared purpose—rather than retreating into Washington's selfish tradition of zero-sum politics. They need to accept that every human being deserves to be listened to. You have ideas and opinions that I should listen to, and I have ideas and opinions that I want you to hear. Together, we should be able to come up with a better alternative based on our holistic and shared knowledge. That's the way it *should* work in Congress and the White House: actual, interactive, respectful conversations that start with listening and understanding the other side.

A professor from Georgetown University developed my favorite exercise from the Presidential Leadership Scholars program. It was called "Five Farmers." We were divided into groups of six, and each of us received a piece of paper that included a series of nonsensical facts. We were not allowed to look at others' papers, and we couldn't take notes. We were tasked with answering two simple questions in twenty minutes:

1. Who is driving the truck?
2. Who is growing the apples?

It might sound childish, but you'd probably be amazed at how difficult this problem proved to be.

I remember the professor saying, "The greatest lesson you can take from this is that you probably don't have all the information you need to solve the problem." Only by listening to and talking with others could we come up with a solution. All the answers were at the table. You had to listen to everyone speak. You had to set aside your preconceived notions and answers, and then you could eventually arrive at a synergistic conclusion based on the observations of listening to and respecting one another.

Believe it or not, and to the best of my knowledge, that group of sixty Presidential Leadership scholars couldn't come up with the correct answers in 2015.

The exercise was so powerful that I made it a go-to tool in my consulting business and have administered it to groups of employees from corporations across the country for the past ten years. Watching different groups try to come up with a solution is sometimes hilarious. There is often an alpha male who tries to take over the room, and there are passive people who don't contribute in any way. In some cases, discussions become quite heated and lead to arguments because the sides can't decide who is right and who is wrong. Too many times, there is only one answer and no middle ground.

Surprisingly, one of the few groups to arrive at the correct answers over the past decade was a collection of high school seniors. They patiently read the facts on their pieces of paper to one another, listened intently, and then came to the answers together. My guess is they were successful because they didn't have preconceived notions about other people in the room—they hadn't yet turned into controlling adults. Solving the problem came down to holding loosely to preconceived notions and coming to the third alternative by using everyone's information and working together. It's amazing what you can accomplish if you simply let your guard down, open your mind, listen to others, and work collectively to find a third way.

I was assigned a personal life coach as part of the Presidential Leadership Scholars program. I'm not sure if the program's leaders were trying to be funny or not, but they decided to put the Texas pastor with a practicing Hindu. I sat across the table from her for three or four sessions, and by the end of that time, we came to know each other pretty well. Through our conversations, she came to respect my convictions, and I respected where she was coming from, even though we had sharply different views about our respective faiths.

Americans must begin to understand that the extremes in religion and politics gain followers and power through fear. When people face uncertainty and the unknown, they obviously want something certain and tangible to hold on to. When life is changing all around us at a rapid pace, uncertainty and fear of what's coming next create a vacuum where certainty once resided. That's when leaders of the extremes step in and pounce on our insecurities.

At certain points during my decades in ministry and theological study, people asked questions about topics that were once considered "settled matters" of theology. Believe me, those who were threatened by someone's curiosity were quick to label them as heretics and rally the troops against them.

Most of us grew up with the notion that there was no such thing as a dumb question, but as we became adults, we discovered that this maxim isn't always true. In reality, there *are* certain subjects that aren't open for discussion, and if you dare bring them up, the extremes come out of the woodwork to shut you down.

I encountered the same dynamics during my short time in politics. Having served as mayor of a major fossil fuel center, I can think of no better example than climate change. Over the past two decades, it seems there are only two accepted theories when it comes to global warming: the settled science of climate change, or you're a crazy climate-change denier. There are those two extremes and nothing else in between.

The truth is that science is never "settled" and is endlessly evolving, and a culture that seeks the pursuit of truth should remain curious without being labeled "science deniers." Unfortunately, there doesn't seem to be a place in America for productive discussions about climate change, where we can learn from one another with humility and possibly discover a new, third way to care for our environment while still having the resources we need to survive on Earth. Instead, people on both sides of the argument are unwilling to listen to one another.

In January 2021, I was invited to appear on *PBS News Hour* to discuss then-President Joe Biden's planned series of executive orders tackling the climate crisis in America and around the world. Biden would eventually direct the Secretary of the Interior Department to stop new oil and natural gas leases on public lands and waters and to review existing leases for fossil fuel development. Biden had already halted construction of the Keystone XL pipeline, and he also wanted to find ways for America to double offshore wind production by 2030.

When *PBS News Hour* host Judy Woodruff asked for my reaction to President Biden's energy proposal, I told her that we had more than two hundred thousand people working in the oil and gas industry and wind and solar sectors in the Permian Basin. "Out here, we realize that it's really going to be 'all the above' as we move forward into the twenty-first century," I said. "So, while China will burn more coal today than the rest of the civilized world, we out here know what it takes to build a robust energy economy and what it's going to take to create those jobs. We're already doing that in the wind and solar environment. We also know that, for us to have the power grid we're going to have for you to plug in your electric vehicle and get it charged, it's going to take the oil and gas industry."[118]

More than anything else, I told Woodruff, I wanted the Biden administration and federal legislators to conduct inclusive conversations about energy and stop unfairly demonizing the oil and gas industry. "I think part of that is because legislators know it's going to require an all-in effort, and not a demonization effort of either side," I said. "So, we will see if we can move forward with a wholehearted discussion covering all the issues, and no longer demonizing the industry that makes it possible for you to carry your Nalgene bottle and wear your Patagonia clothes while, at the same time, you can drive your electric vehicle."[119]

Bill Peduto, the then-mayor of Pittsburgh, Pennsylvania, also appeared on the show and boasted of his city's efforts to invest in the "inevitable transformation into renewable energy and green technology."

"Look, Pittsburgh is where oil was discovered at the Drake Well just north of our city," Peduto said. "Coal was discovered along the shores of our Monongahela River. We sit at one of the largest reserves of natural gas in the world. And yet there's more jobs in green and renewable energy than oil, gas, and coal combined."[120]

With all due respect to Peduto, a Democrat who served as Pittsburgh's mayor from 2014 to 2022, his last statement wasn't close to being true. "I think the Democrat left has demonized the oil and gas industry from the far extreme left side," I said. "So, we will see if Mr. Biden in his conversation of unity really means that. And that's going to take both sides to get their radical sides out of the debate and get in the middle and have this discussion."[121]

After that conversation, I ended up appearing on BBC and talking about energy again. I simply repeated the same things: Debate was healthy, and reasonable people can come up with reasonable solutions for the good of everyone. I would have loved to sit down with Mayor Peduto over a beer and have an honest discussion with him about finding the appropriate balance between economics and climate change.

Despite what you might have heard, it doesn't take much for opposing sides to come together and find a collective solution. Countless times while I served as the mayor of Midland, people came to the city council with what seemed to be intractable situations involving zoning, planning, or construction. Whether it was a builder looking to construct a new home in a residential area or a commercial builder seeking a zoning variance, the city council would oftentimes send them back to the drawing board to find an answer on their own. Remarkably, I can't recall a single instance in which the opposing parties didn't come back to us with an agreeable compromise.

After I decided to run for public office, I sat in on several city council meetings to see how the then-mayor operated. I took notes as I formulated my campaign strategy. During one meeting, there was a heated debate about imposing impact fees, which are essentially taxes on builders to help pay for new infrastructure like road, water towers, and sewer lines needed to accommodate development. The discussion between the builders and the mayor became contentious. At that point, the mayor said, "Well, we've already decided, regardless of what you guys think." He slammed down his gavel and the meeting was over.

The next day, I called the spokesman for the developers and asked if we could meet. I asked him, "What just happened?"

"Well, the only thing I know is that you'll have my vote because you were willing to have a conversation and try to come to a better way for everybody," the builder said. "Once the finger was pointed at us and we were told there's no alternative, we were done. We agree that impact fees are necessary in a rapidly growing city like Midland, but if you're not willing to talk to us about how to best implement them, then we're not going to be able to do what's best for the city."

Impact fees ended up being one of the issues that helped get me across the finish line in the mayoral election.

Many people have asked me how I came up with the idea of the Middle. For nearly four decades, Covey's words about synergy have been maturing in my soul. Year after year, my aversion to the extremes has grown as the far left and far right continue to inflict serious damage to our country. There were times when I found myself thinking like someone on the far edges. I had to humble myself and admit that I often see the world not as *it* was, but only as *I* was. I had to escape the fear of new ideas and new ways of thinking—and especially new ways of seeing people—if

I was ever going to start down a path that would be prosperous for everyone.

We will never see a movement of the majority middle until we have a personal revival of brave humility in our neighborhoods, churches, city halls, state houses, and Washington, DC. It will take great courage to cease judging people as I am and start seeing people as they are—and what we can do together.

Jesus actually tells us to stop looking at the speck in our brother's eye and ignoring the log in our own. This doesn't mean we cannot be judicious in our observations and interactions, but it does remind us that if we are to honor one another and benefit our society with better relationships and ideas, we must first take a look in the mirror and begin with ourselves rather than demanding much of others.

The third way starts by asking better questions and listening intently—and resisting the all too familiar comfort of choosing sides. It begins not in Congress or state capitols but around kitchen tables, in classrooms, in how we treat our neighbors. The third way isn't the easiest path, but it's clearly the best one.

CHAPTER 15

Risky Liberty

While you might believe the current political climate in America is as bad as it has ever been—and that there's little chance that the sensible people in our country can bring the extremes back to the Middle—you might be surprised to learn that we've been down this road many times throughout our history. And we've somehow managed to come out on the other side.

Gideon Rose, an adjunct senior fellow at the Council on Foreign Relations, noted that the current political climate in the United States is much like—or at least feels like—it was, believe it or not, in the 1790s and 1850s. Less than two decades after the country's founding, conservative Federalists and libertarian Republicans attacked each other viciously as they fought over the direction the world's first independent constitutional democracy would take. Rose wrote:

The fights were so vicious in part because the stakes were so high. Americans were doing something nobody had done before, ever—simultaneously creating a single country out of thirteen disparate colonies, establishing a continent-sized republic, and giving a large swath of the population the vote. An entirely new polity was being designed on the fly, and everything was up for grabs: the players, the teams, even the rules of the game itself.[122]

Even though the telegraph and telephone hadn't been invented yet, "partisan tabloids filled with diatribes and disinformation" stirred the voting public to choose sides and "turned politics into an all-encompassing culture war," according to Rose.[123] Eventually, the Thomas Jefferson–led Democratic-Republicans and Alexander Hamilton–led Federalists worked together and found common ground.

Six decades later, America's partisan division reached a breaking point when western expansion caused the nation to finally tackle its ugly question about slavery. When Republican Abraham Lincoln was elected to the White House in 1861, Southern states seceded, leading to the bloody Civil War. Like now, the warring factions couldn't decide on even the most fundamental issues of humanity.

"The country is not at risk of political collapse or civil war, and has, however slowly, improved dramatically over the long run," Rose wrote. "Yet somehow it is still replicating the toxic political psychology and extreme emotions of the lowest period in its national history. It is not the 1850s. But it feels as bad."[124]

Jefferson's "grand experiment" was an ambitious notion that a country could be built on the foundation of liberty—that ordinary people could govern themselves without kings or ruling elites calling the shots. Jefferson and the other Founding Fathers chose liberty over security, giving the nation's citizens the freedom to state their opinions, challenge the government, vote for the candidates of their choosing, and chart their own futures as long as they didn't harm others.

Of course, liberty came with monumental risks, and the founders had to find a delicate balance between individual freedom and its potential impact on society as a whole. James Madison, The "Father of the Constitution" and the fourth US president, was so alarmed about the potential rise of mob rule and political factions that he and others supported the separation of powers—safeguards still in our federal government today.

The Middle views life and liberty as filled with undiscovered opportunity rather than a zero-sum game with clear winners and losers. The voice of the Middle is found outside the halls of the elite and the ruling classes. Throughout our history, the common theme of the ruling class and those in power was that the common man could not possibly know what was best for him. Peasants and others were granted few rights and certainly were not considered capable of the gift of self-governance. Then, the great miracle of self-governance, life, and liberty emerged in America. This risk of liberty was built on the assumption—the belief—that virtuous and free people are capable of self-governance and don't need the ruling or elected class to know what's best for them. This liberty also assumed a free and virtuous people would know how to self-govern. This risky liberty means a number of things, if we are going to recover the necessary voice, power, and country in the Middle.

This idea and practice of risky liberty is anathema to the extremes' ringleaders. The extremes want to gain or maintain control for their own position and power. The systems and structures of leadership in governance, both in ecclesiology and politics, are formed and operated for control rather than freedom and liberty. Whether it was the Founding Fathers of America or the apostle Paul, we are reminded that it was for freedom we have been created.

Liberty is not the brazen disrespect of law and order but rather the values-driven pursuit of what is good for self and others. Liberty is not to be separated from morality, but it is within morality that liberty and freedom flourish. Our Founding Fathers knew that only a virtuous people could truly live at liberty, for without virtue and morality, we are prone to slide into selfishness, which quickly bypasses care and love of one another.

Nevertheless, to choose to cherish and live in liberty also requires that I accept the practice of liberty in others. This means a freedom of thought and expression that can make me uncomfortable. I may not like the choices others make, but within a free people of virtue that honors one another, we are able to choose our path of belief and practice.

There's arrogance in a world in which the extremes take control. The extremes talk with an authoritative voice, demanding that their rivals be silenced, while their side gains audience and control. The Middle must call out the vitriol of the extremes and embrace the diversity and voice of a common humanity—knit together by the American dream of liberty, not the despotic demands of the extremes.

The extremes are driven by a sense of what they can control and what they might lose if they don't win their chosen battle. This assertion holds true regardless of the issue at hand and which side we're looking at. The radical left is afraid the radical right will take away their rights of self-expression and reproductive freedom. The radical right is convinced the radical left will doom this country to atheism and Marxism.

The Middle views life and liberty as filled with undiscovered opportunity rather than a zero-sum game with clear winners and losers. History is littered with kings and kingdoms that viewed life and statehood as a zero-sum game in order to protect the power gained by the extreme elites. This great nation was not built for one side to win and the other to lose but rather for all sides to work together toward one goal: our shared pursuit of life, liberty, and happiness. However, we distract ourselves by focusing not on the goal but on how *our side* views the pursuit and what life, liberty, and happiness must look like *from our own extreme position.*

It cannot be underestimated how much the systems and structures of our current religious and political extremes seek to control and restrict the true practice of liberty. The Republican and Democrat parties are both vast machines of conformity built and maintained by the party leadership—galvanized by their systems and structures of money and position.

One need look no further than the circular and nonproductive discussions about immigration. Over the past decades, party systems and structures have dictated the respective narratives of both parties, so that nothing is done to improve or reform immigration policy. The extremes grab the framing of the difficult issues and work against true liberty of thought and discussion that can lead to new and better pathways, while the majority middle wonders why progress seems so difficult and the extremes get louder and louder.

In the world of religion, the large denominations and their power structures stand guard over the truth with their own set of systems and structures. The liberty promised by the gospel is lost in the systems and structures that fear the life of liberty promised to the laity. Who hasn't heard the rules and regulations of any faith community that must be upheld to maintain good standing within the ecclesiastical structures of various religious groups?

I can remember the endless lists of what you could not do, say, or think—and especially what you could not call into question—if you were going to fit into the restrictive path prescribed by the extremes of religious systems and structures. Of course, there were always relevant matters of behavior and action that one should consider and practice wisely, but the yoke of control within the walls of houses of worship consistently protected the congregation from the risky liberty of those who might choose to ask questions and dare to think differently. This extreme desire to control liberty is centuries old, as even the apostle Paul wrote to the early church to remind them, "For freedom Christ has set us free; stand firm therefore, and do not submit again to a yoke of slavery" (Galatians 5:1).

Extremes do not like and do not foster the radical pursuit of liberty because liberty is at the heart of exploring and discovering the promise and benefits of life and happiness. A free people are a dangerous people because they demand accountability from those in power for the ones they claim to serve, yet upon closer observation, these leaders seek to restrict freedoms for their own benefit and control.

This call to embrace risky liberty might be one of the more challenging issues the Middle will face as it seeks to push back against the extremes that continue to divide us into warring camps. At its very core, liberty carries seeds of conflict but also the opportunity to respect and honor.

If we are going to recover the power and promise nurtured by the American dream that is locked up in the hearts and minds of the Middle, we must be willing once again to foster and promote the richness of thinking and discussion that investigates the curiosity of others and seeks to understand one another. That's the only way we'll find alternative paths to prosperity and processes that unleash our creative spirit toward a shared American dream.

One of the cherished principles of America is the freedom and free practice of religion. At its very core, this promise ensures that people are never governed by the extremes of any religion or practice and can freely choose their religious practices or lack thereof.

After George Washington was elected the first president of the newly formed United States in 1789, he toured the country to unify what were once the thirteen colonies. Several religious groups wrote him letters, expressing their desires that they not face discrimination from the new federal government, including the Touro Synagogue in Newport, Rhode Island, which was the oldest Hebrew congregation in America.

In Washington's response to the Touro Synagogue, he famously quoted Hebrew Scriptures: "May the children of the stock of Abraham who dwell in this land continue to merit and enjoy the good will of the other inhabitants—while every one shall sit in safety under his own vine and fig tree and there shall be none to make him afraid."[125] Specifically, Washington cited Micah 4:4: "But they shall all sit under their own vines and under their own fig trees, and no one shall make them afraid."[126]

Since many colonists had fled religious tyranny, Washington assured them that the new government would not only tolerate them but would protect their rights in matters of conscience and belief: "The Government of the United States . . . gives to bigotry no sanction, to persecution no assistance."[127]

The extremes on the left and the right seem to enjoy invoking the support of God Almighty in their divisive arguments. The extremes use God and religion in their arguments for immigration. The extremes use God and religion for their arguments surrounding pregnancy and abortion. The extremes use God and religion for their arguments regarding prayer and Bible studies in schools.

Every person on the extremes seems to think that if they can use God and religion for their side, the matter is closed, and debate should end on the claims of God and religion. But these very claims and arguments are based on personal and institutional interpretations of sacred text and practice. Although at times well-meaning, these dangerous practices galvanize groups and discourage conversation, dialogue, and understanding, which then undermines our practice of risky liberty and the flourishing of freedoms.

It takes a people of great virtue to respect others' religious and life differences in such a way that a kaleidoscope of people and practice can thrive in the Middle rather than being controlled by the fear created by the extremes. As I have mentioned throughout this book, the extremes thrive where fear of loss and uncertainty prevail. But it is only through our conversations in which uncertainty is most immense that we can seek to understand other viewpoints and honor the risky liberty of life and practices of others.

As mayor of Midland, I remember countless emails and text messages from people claiming what "God would have me do" on seemingly every issue, from COVID-19 restrictions to building codes. Their claims on behalf of God were almost always bent toward an ordinance or practice that would shut down one argument and exalt another; rarely did their holy proclamations foster freedom and liberty.

Despite the divine arguments on both sides of the issues, I tried to stick to the middle road. For example, regarding COVID-19, I continued telling the people of our city to consult with their families and doctors and then choose the best health practices for themselves. The response was predictable: One side told me I was being un-Christian by not obeying state and federal guidelines, and the other side told me I was being un-Christian by not promoting individual freedom and trusting God's protection from the virus.

In the end, I knew I could not violate the risky liberty that is the gift of the American dream and promise. I knew in my soul that the extremes were in full-tilt mode in this historic season of uncertainty, and the promise of liberty was too much for the extremes to handle.

It was a promise and path that had nurtured our great country for more than two centuries—and history had taught me that virtuous liberty is a greater guide than the control and virtue-signaling each extreme was clamoring for.

CHAPTER 16

Yes, It's Love

While I was the mayor of Midland, the federal government sent about seven hundred immigrant children to a temporary overflow holding facility at the site of a former camp for oil field workers. Immediately, Midland's citizens were up in arms, saying we were being "invaded" by Mexico.

Amid this uproar, I drove out to take a look at the camp. The federal government had placed black tarps on the fencing so people couldn't see inside. I felt a duty as mayor to know what was happening to the children inside and demanded a tour.

Even before that visit, I must say that my opinions were already forming around the invasion narrative, mostly because we were receiving so little communication from the federal government. As the media and citizens galvanized around the extreme notion that illegal immigrants were overrunning us, the only way

I could find out the actual truth was to go see the camp myself. As a leader of the city, I wanted to find a way to understand before haphazardly reacting.

I talked to a doctor who was treating many of the children. He told me that many of the kids' feet were blistered from walking thousands of miles. He said some of them had recent incisions from selling their kidneys to pay traffickers to get them across the border. The most treacherous part of their journey was the last half mile, crossing the Rio Grande River. Some of them arrived in the US with the names and phone numbers of relatives to contact once they were here.

That visit gave me a deeper understanding of human trafficking and the pain and suffering of thousands of people. I went on the radio and found a way to reframe the debate because it had been so radicalized by extremes on both sides. I told the audience that immigration isn't about being right or wrong—it's about the common humanity we shared in saving these children. It's not a left and right debate—it's about humanity. It's about *love*.

In this particular case, it was about innocent children in desperate need of help. I wasn't ignoring the national debate around open or closed borders, nor the venomous rhetoric coming out of the Texas state capital or Washington, DC. Instead, I sought first to understand before taking the easy route of attacking people and situations I had no firsthand knowledge about.

The Middle is built on the foundation of love. In the words of Robert Greenleaf, "Love is . . . unlimited liability."[128] Love is a commitment we make to one another that believes all things, hopes all things, and endures all things. Love is the understanding that, as the great apostle Paul reminded us, "we see in a mirror dimly" (1 Corinthians 13:12). We must, therefore, see love as the bedrock principle to all the other principles.

The genius of the American way of life and governance is the acknowledgment that all of us have been equally created, but this created status does not then demand singular expression outside of respect and honor. The door is wide open for diversity of opinion and practice, but love is the hinge that keeps it from coming off the wall of respect and honor for one another. Loving thy neighbor is about having mutual respect and understanding and cultivating harmonious relationships with people of different beliefs and backgrounds. Both sides in America seem to have an uncontrollable urge to claim God as being "on their side." From immigration to welfare to social justice to the environment, God is the favorite additive to every speech, cause, and legislation. Yet both sides seem to skip the part about their works speaking louder than their words and loving enemies even more than we love our friends, as espoused by Jesus Himself in the Sermon on the Mount.

The Middle realizes that every world religion has some form of the Golden Rule: "Whatever you wish that others would do to you, do also to them" (Matthew 7:12). This principle is not exclusive to evangelicals or the larger Judeo-Christian community.

In Judaism, it's expressed in Talmud, Shabbat 31a: "What is hateful to you, do not do to your fellow."

In Islam, a hadith of the Prophet Muhammad says, "None of you truly believes until he wishes for his brother what he wishes for himself."

The Middle

In Buddhism, the Golden Rule is conveyed in Udana-Varga 5.18: "Treat not others in ways that you yourself would find hurtful."

And in Hinduism, it's revealed in Mahabharata 5:1517: "This is the sum of duty: do not do to others what would cause pain if done to you."

Somewhere along the line in America, cynicism and doubt about our fellow man overtook optimism, trust, and hope. Too often, we cover others with labels rather than love. We need more love in our world—not the type of love that we read about in mushy romance novels, but a love that begins with wanting the best for others because we would want others to want the best for us.

Unfortunately, this call to love is almost always met with an immediate defense as thick as castle walls, rooted in anger over what the other side supposedly did or said. That resentment becomes exacerbated over time through the constant drumbeat of outrageous opinions from so-called experts on cable and main-stream media networks and social media. When we were kids, our parents taught us not to talk to strangers to keep us safe. Now, we're being told by our colleagues, friends, and political leaders that we can't be nice to people who have opinions that differ from ours. That's a dangerous way to live.

This slide into constant fear, doubt, and cynicism has infected nearly every interaction Americans have in everyday life, from politics to religion and even to Little League baseball fields, where disagreements with a volunteer umpire sometimes spiral into inexcusable violence. The extremes are killing us, and we must find a way back to respect and honor.

Yes, It's Love

As a pastor, I have facilitated hundreds of weddings. Of course, no wedding ceremony is complete without reading the following words of the apostle Paul:

> Love is patient and kind; love does not envy or boast; it is not arrogant or rude. It does not insist on its own way; it is not irritable or resentful; it does not rejoice at wrongdoing, but rejoices with the truth. Love bears all things, believes all things, hopes all things, endures all things. Love never ends. . . . So now faith, hope, and love abide, these three; but the greatest of these is love. (1 Corinthians 13:4–8, 13)

For over two decades, I have read these words to soon-to-be husbands and wives, yet it was only a few years ago when I happened to notice the words of the apostle Paul that are sandwiched in the middle of this thirteen-verse chapter in the Bible. Even though it is a short passage, the words gave me fresh insight into the calling that love also demands of us.

Paul wrote in 1 Corinthians,

> As for prophecies, they will pass away; as for tongues, they will cease; as for knowledge, it will pass away. For we know in part. . . . When I was a child, I spoke like a child, I thought like a child, I reasoned like a child. When I became a man, I gave up childish ways. For now we see in a mirror dimly. (13:8–9, 11–12)

The Middle

You don't have to be an evangelical or even particularly religious to pay attention to ancient words of wisdom and guidance. Remember the earlier point about all world religions saying something similar in the admonition to love one another? In the context of a famous chapter about love in the Bible, the old apostle included a line about humility that we would do well to note if we are truly trying to live our lives among others. The line of humility tells us, "For now we see in a mirror dimly" (v. 12). In these eight words, we are reminded that we can't see the entire picture. And to add weight to his point, Paul preceded these eight words with a reminder of how children act.

What adult hasn't listened to a child, teenager, or even a young adult talk about life as if they knew everything about the world and had experienced everything in life? Most of the time, out of familial or friendly respect and love, we let them speak as experts, while reminding ourselves how we once thought with such certainty until life taught us otherwise. Only a foolish friend or parent would respond to such juvenile confidence by saying, "You are such a fool!"

We remember what it was like to think and act as a child and eventually learn to give up naive thinking wrapped in certainty. Through the trials and tribulations of adulthood, we learned life was going to throw curveballs into our way of thinking. In the words of Paul, we begin to understand with age and maturity that our certainty was often clouded, and we still had much to learn.

For my friends of religious conviction, this type of "cloudy certainty" is often difficult to work through. They are certain of their convictions and even more so of who taught them and the inerrant nature of the source of their convictions. I understand this thinking but also realize that much of what we are certain of is based on interpretation, which is rarely without bias. Our own "inerrant" texts are telling us our sight is cloudy.

For my friends on the political extremes, this invitation into the reality of cloudy thinking is equally difficult. Their life experiences and rooted trust in left- or right-wing voices hold such certainty and protection from the other side that they find it hard to believe they are anything but 100 percent correct in their view of the political landscape.

I find it interesting when I approach evangelicals with the idea that they never would have supported Donald Trump in the presidential elections if he had run as a Democrat. They would have called him a casino-building, womanizing man lacking moral scruples. These same evangelical extremes were ready to run former President Bill Clinton out of office for his illicit behavior in the Oval Office, but nearly three decades later, we're willing to turn a blind eye to similar behaviors for the overall cause.

More than anything else, Trump held up their extreme desire to be a voice and sledgehammer against the other extreme—the left—so they were more than willing to carry his water. Not to be outdone, the left constantly said former President George W. Bush was unfit for office because he couldn't complete a sentence, which was clearly plaguing President Joe Biden at the end of his tenure in the White House.

If the right discusses cutting budgets to reduce the federal deficit, the far left pulls out the old trope of the far right wanting to kill grandma. All this is a symptom of fanaticism that drives foolishness. This fanaticism always protects, guards, and defends so blindly and violently that it loses sight of our shared humanity and the personhood of others. The Middle is tired of this symphony of the absurd. We have to love our neighbors and so-called enemies and actually work to understand the other side.

For the most part, the extreme right latched onto Trump because they saw him as a voice and force against the radical left, while the far left hitched its wagons to Biden and Vice President Kamala Harris because they viewed them as a protection against the extreme right. In the end, both Democrats and Republicans found and supported candidates to guard and protect the opinions and positions of the extremes. Both sides need to offer some unlimited liability to themselves and to others so they might gain a helping hand to see more clearly through the lenses of another.

As a former politician and preacher, I have had conversations with others about hotly debated topics: taxes, immigration, abortion, LGBTQ+ rights, public education, global warming, and even whether a youth soccer team should be allowed to practice on Sunday. In all these conversations, there have been areas of intense disagreement and occasional agreement. In nearly every one of these instances, I had to learn to approach the conversation with the thought: *The person I am speaking with is created in the image of God and deserves all respect and love first.*

When I followed that heartfelt conviction, I then reminded myself that my glasses are dirty and I needed help in seeing better.

The only way to see better is to share and compare cloudy viewpoints. Over the years, I can say this cloudy practice of love has protected me from my own extremes and challenged the extremes of others, while still affording us both the chance to see and be heard. In many instances, I became friends with the people who had opposing views.

The decades-long growth of the extremes in America has been built on a foundation of cloudy certainty that has capitalized on a population wandering fearfully in the abyss because of its own dim vision. Many Americans have naively assumed the loudest voices of the extremes have somehow found certainty.

The Middle realizes that no one has a corner on the market of perfect vision. Somehow, we must view one another with the certainty of our humanity instead of through the cloudy vision of our differing viewpoints and opinions. Only then can we better navigate the winding road of life, liberty, and happiness. If people with cloudy vision take this walk together, we can find our way along this path without running into the painful walls of the extremes.

True love is loaded with risk and even fear. When you fall in love with the one who becomes your life partner, there is always a sense of the unknown in the back of your mind that makes you uneasy. Only true love endures and makes taking the risk worth it.

Who among us who loves a particular sports team hasn't had to deal with the risk of our team letting us down? We hope for a better day and give our team "unlimited liability" for another day of optimism and winning. Love requires risk, and risk demands that we engage one another with humility and grace, or the extremes will tear us apart through fear and pride.

Even if we find it hard to love one another, we must understand that loving this country requires us to love our neighbor and truly see one another as neighbors rather than enemies.

CHAPTER 17

Get in the Game

If the Middle is going to retake America from the extremes on both sides of the aisle, we must get back in the game of governance. It has been easier for Americans to check out than to check back in for far too long. The Middle must choose to either engage or reengage. As President Dwight D. Eisenhower once famously said, "We must avoid extremes, for vacillation between extremes is inefficient, costly, and destructive of morale."[129]

Whether it's on Main Street or K Street, those living in the Middle must become more active. Run for a seat on the school board in your community and hold ground in the middle rather than in the extremes. Take an even more ambitious step and run for election at the city or state levels, and for a season dig in your heels on the issues that matter most to you—regardless of how your political party leadership might be telling you to vote. Cross the street and meet your neighbors, who might have an opposing political candidate's sign in their lawn. Have an adult discussion with them about politics and America.

Above all, the Middle must regain its backbone and stand its ground in what is becoming an increasingly uncomfortable world. People find their identity in extremes when they perceive them as a safe place from the other side. The reality is that the extremes were the crazy ones until they kept hammering away at the fringes. Now their ideologies seem mainstream in a country searching for its lost identity.

The Middle must hammer away and stand its ground until the tide turns and the majority middle regains the mainstream of what it means to pursue life, liberty, and happiness in America.

We would do well in this ongoing crisis to consider an excerpt from one of President Theodore Roosevelt's speeches. On April 23, 1910, while at the Sorbonne in Paris, Roosevelt gave a speech titled "Citizenship in a Republic," which, over time, has simply been referred to as "The Man in the Arena." While the entire transcript is worth reading, I think this excerpt speaks specifically to the matter at hand:

> It is not the critic who counts; not the man who points out how the strong man stumbles, or where the doer of deeds could have done them better. The credit belongs to the man who is actually in the arena, whose face is marred by dust and sweat and blood; who strives valiantly; who errs, who comes short again and again, because there is no effort without error and shortcoming; but who

does actually strive to do the deeds; who knows great enthusiasms, the great devotions; who spends himself in a worthy cause; who at the best knows in the end the triumph of high achievement, and who at the worst, if he fails, at least fails while daring greatly, so that his place shall never be with those cold and timid souls who neither know victory nor defeat.[130]

Our time in history is marked by the critic who can pound out vitriol, animosity, complaints, and gripes with little to no accountability, and with an assumption by the keyboard and media warriors that their opinions and grievances should carry the day and make a difference. The fundamental problem with our keyboard wars and sound-bite battles is that while the number of complaints grows and the noise gets louder, real solutions never keep pace.

I believe this problem is a direct result of a widespread misconception in America—that simply posting on social media and talking loudly about certain issues will make a real difference in solving our greatest problems. They don't, and they won't.

The only way we'll solve our greatest challenges is to get up from behind the keyboard, stop relying on social media, turn away from our growing addiction to algorithm-driven media, and personally get in the game.

But what do I mean by getting in the game?

During my time as mayor, I was a guest on local talk radio shows every other week or so to discuss the city council, governance, and important local issues. For the longest time, one of the top three complaints I received from citizens through phone calls and texts while on air was what the city was going to do about the growing problem of litter on our roads and parks.

Well, I've long believed that you don't get to complain about something unless you're willing to do something about it. So, I started answering every call and text with the following reply: "If you want to see something done about litter and trash, then start picking up litter and trash and ask others to help you."

Before long, the calls and text messages stopped, and the radio station even challenged its listeners to pick up two pieces of trash a day. The only thing I did was encourage people to be part of the solution. It doesn't matter whether it was their fault or not; it was our problem collectively, and it was on each of us to get in the game and find a solution.

Of course, the issues that plague America and threaten to fracture us beyond healing are not all as simple as picking up trash. But the principle to fix our current political climate remains the same: Stop complaining unless you're willing to get in the game. But realize, in the spirit of this entire book, that getting in the game means dealing with our issues *with* one another rather than *through* one another.

I had two rules while I was the pastor of Stonegate Fellowship Church in Midland:

1. I would never open mail that did not have a return name and address clearly visible on the envelope, and likewise, I wouldn't open or respond to an email by an anonymous person.

2. I would listen to complaints only if people were willing to help find an answer to the problem and be part of the solution.

Over time, and with a growing mountain of emails, I modified these rules to the point where I would pay attention to a complainant's email only if he or she was willing to have a phone call or personal meeting. If they wouldn't talk or meet with me, I was done with them. I know some might view that as being overly harsh or inconsiderate. I can already hear longtime church members saying, "But as pastor, you should listen to it all and pay attention to it all!" I understand that sentiment.

The point of my actions was to encourage people to grow from being complainers to fixers who are willing to get things done. If you're not willing to engage the matter that bothers you so much, then you're not that serious about fixing the problem. Like President Roosevelt said, you must get in the arena. But beware—more fans than fighters surround the arena.

To this day, I keep two types of boxes in my office. What was once a pair of boxes has grown into a half dozen over the years. What's in these boxes? Copies of two types of correspondence: hate mail and letters of encouragement. I don't keep all my anonymous hate mail (remember what I said about anonymous senders), but I keep enough to remind me of what some people are thinking and saying. And I keep encouragement boxes because sometimes you need to reread messages from people who appreciate your time in the arena.

Why tell you this? Simple: If you choose to get in the game, you're going to be criticized by others who might not agree with you. It's part of being in the arena. It's why there are more fans than people playing the game. Remember the quote often attributed to British Prime Minister Winston Churchill, who knew a thing or two about being in the arena: "You have enemies? Good. That means you've stood up for something, sometime in your life."

So, what should you do to get in the game?

Stop Complaining

Make a commitment to stop complaining unless you're willing to do something about it. We have enough negativity surrounding us every day. Don't add to the world's misery. This will be difficult for some people because we've lost touch with just how much we complain. Remember what the American humorist Mark Twain said about complaining (or at least the quote is attributed to him): "Don't complain and talk about all your problems—80 percent of people don't care; the other 20 percent are glad you have them."

Whether it's about waiters and waitresses at local restaurants, volunteer youth coaches, or politicians on TV, some of us have views and opinions we think the world needs to hear. Too many people turn every small inconvenience into a Shakespearean tragedy. I've got news for you: Your complaining has never solved a problem, drawn people together, or moderated the extremes. Try the no-complaining rule for just one day and see how difficult it is. This rule applies to conversations on all fronts—in person, on cell phones, in emails, in text messages, and, yes, even social media.

When you find yourself surrounded by complainers, handle them with grace and humility. After listening to Negative Nancy and Gloomy Gus try to ruin your day, ask them the following question: "I respect your opinion about this matter that you seem very passionate about. What do you suggest we do about it to make it better or solve the problem?"

One final note on the no-complaining rule: You'll probably have lapses, but don't give up. Acknowledge your mistake and recommit to the rule.

Put Up or Shut Up

Volunteer at an organization that focuses on the issues that matter to you. No matter what areas might concern you—whether it's the homeless, the environment, poverty, or education—I promise there are groups out there that are trying to make things better. All you must do is be willing to find them and give your time.

If you're convinced the schools in your area need to improve, then sign up for the local Parent Teacher Association. Even better, meet with administrators and ask where they need help. Organize efforts to address those problems. Don't make your first meeting with administrators your moment to complain like an extremist. Instead, show up to serve and earn the right to be trusted and heard.

If you're interested in local government and public policy, stop watching cable TV news and get involved with the local branch of your political party of choice. Show up with a curious mind and find ways to serve people, not just sit and complain about them. Attend city council meetings and volunteer on a political campaign. Join a citizen advisory board and campaign for issues that matter to you.

Be Curious

Demonstrate curiosity. We talked about being curious in a previous chapter, but applying the practice in your day-to-day life might be more difficult. You must make a commitment to learning all you can about issues and other people, and that takes time, patience, and plenty of questions.

One of the great leadership teachers of the past several decades has been author and pastor John Maxwell. I have had several opportunities to hear him speak, and I've even sat privately with him. I've been amazed at the number of questions John asks when he is around people. He always seems genuinely curious about everyone in the room. Maybe that's why he once said: "The greatest enemy of learning is knowing."[131]

I promise you that John has learned more in his nearly eight decades on earth than most people, but his humility and deep desire to listen have been an incredible example to me of what it looks and sounds like to be curious, ask questions, and learn from others.

Bottom line: Getting involved means becoming curious.

Serve Before Being Served

Seek to serve before demanding to be served.

On January 20, 1961, new President John F. Kennedy famously told America to do exactly that in his inaugural address: "Ask not what your country can do for you—ask what you can do for your country."[132] Repeat JFK's words over and over again to fully understand what it's going to take for our country to pull itself back from the extremes and find common good in the Middle.

Instead of worrying about what we want and what others can give us, imagine how much we could accomplish in America if everyone's initial thought was, *What can I do?* What if our first reaction to others was based on how we can serve them instead of how we're going to react to what they've said or what they're doing?

Remember that the extremes are fueled by the words and actions of others—not by an attitude and desire to serve others. The extremes serve only their own and continue to work to create enemies out of the other side. If there is going to be a movement of the Middle, there must be a change toward how we view one another. One certain way to change the way we see and hear one another is by seeking first to serve one another before demanding to be served.

In the days when Jesus walked the earth, people traveled dusty, rocky roads and constantly dealt with dirty feet. Washing people's feet was considered one of the most demeaning tasks, typically reserved for the lowliest servants—never the important or respected figures. But then along came Jesus, and on one fateful evening, He took a towel, wrapped it around His waist, grabbed a tub of water, and began washing His followers' filthy feet as they sat stunned and speechless. If anyone should not be serving by washing feet, it was Jesus. Instead, He gave a lasting example of what it means to love and serve.

If we want to see a movement of the Middle, we must truly desire the dirty work of serving one another. We must demand that every elected official demonstrate a life and leadership of sacrificial service.

The Middle

During my time as a pastor, I was continuously amazed at the ways in which people chose to serve one another. We had a janitor who worked at Stonegate Fellowship Church. I passed him in the hall every day, but I didn't know much about him. During a lunch for staff members, I sat down across from the janitor and said, "Tell me your story."

The janitor's name was Ishmael Villa, and he had been a pastor at Hispanic churches for decades. He and his wife had burned out on the work, so they both decided to take janitorial jobs at our church. At the time, Midland's population was about 60 percent Hispanic, and we had desperately been trying to reach them. Well, sitting right there under my nose was a guy who was content to empty trash and sweep floors and never said a word about his background.

"I think your days of being a janitor are over," I told him.

Ishmael started our outreach work to the Hispanic community in Midland. Eventually, he started his own church and traveled into Mexico doing revivals. He was simply a servant, picking up everyone's trash and never telling anybody about his story. He was a man who would literally take his shirt off his back for you, but you'd never know it unless you had a conversation with him. That's why it's so important to be curious.

As Stonegate Fellowship Church continued to grow, we had massive parking lots surrounding our campus to accommodate thousands of cars and trucks. I needed somebody I could trust to lead our parking team, and Hank Hudson, a man I barely knew, raised his hand to take on the responsibility. Hank showed up every Sunday through rain, sleet, and snow—and his maroon Corvette was typically in the parking lot first. Hank recruited other people to join his parking team. If someone showed up at church who maybe had a difficult background and perhaps believed that a church didn't have any place for him, Hank was sure to recruit him to help.

One of my favorite sayings as a pastor was that the "sermon starts in the parking lot." Hank was a man who lived and died by that statement. I'm sure we've all had difficult Sunday mornings, when you're maybe running late and arguing with the kids to get dressed. Hank was convinced that if he could get to the parking lot early and smile as he waved and gave people directions, he might change somebody's day to have a wonderful time at church. Later, Hank and his wife, Janna, started hosting a dinner for single mothers.

Occasionally, I'd call Hank, and he'd take a day or two to get back to me. He'd call me back from Dubai or some other place in the Middle East. I was aware that Hank was an engineer in the oil and gas industry, but I had no idea that he was one of the world's leading authorities when it came to sulfur recovery and hydrocarbon gas processing. He is the author or coauthor of more than seven hundred patents.

We asked Hank to serve as an officer of the church numerous times, but he declined each time. He preferred to stay in the parking lot, where the sermon started. To this day, you'll see his Corvette in the back of the parking lot at the church, serving people.

Don't give up on the dream of the Founding Fathers' promise: "We hold these truths to be self-evident, that all men are created equal, that they are endowed by their Creator with certain unalienable

Rights, that among these are Life, Liberty and the pursuit of Happiness."[133]

That hope and promise of being an American is not about belonging to a special interest group, race, or religion but rather about believing that the things that might make us different can't stand in the way of the power of a nation made up of moral, virtuous, and united people. Only when we work together can we strive to honor and respect one another for something bigger than any one individual, interest group, or political party.

I don't believe it's an exaggeration to say that America is the greatest country this world has ever known. I believe the reason for this greatness is the wise foundation on which it was built, which rewarded us with a collective power of respectful freedoms. By serving one another and embracing a greater calling of "one Nation under God," we can remain a shining light around the globe.

The extremes believe they're maintaining the promise of America, but the reality is just the opposite. Extremes do not unite us; they divide us and only serve to accomplish narrow and small victories for narrow and small groups. They serve themselves and their select systems and structures of political and religious institutional power. But the extremes have failed to take one thing into account. They've overlooked something—something important, something that endangers their power and threatens their control.

They've lost sight of *us*.

Specifically, the 80 percent of us in the Middle who have had it up to here with the extreme right's and radical left's rhetoric, vitriol, manipulations, divisions, boogeymen, and overall foolishness.

We can't be silent anymore.

We can't let only the loudest and most obnoxious voices control the narratives that drive policy and popular opinion.

We can no longer be run over or pushed aside on the road to America's future.

Today is the day that we, as America's majority middle, must reengage in public discourse, demand service over power, declare love over hate, and finally stand united and truly indivisible as one nation.

Acknowledgments

As this book goes to press I am beyond grateful for those who have made such valuable investments in my life. I think every author and thought leader says the same thing, so let me join the chorus: "Without them this book would never have come to fruition." It is indeed a true statement.

Cindy (my wife): She took the risk of a lifetime when she said yes thirty-six years ago. Many describe me as someone who takes career risks; in hindsight that may be true. But the truth of the matter is every risk I have taken, battle I have chosen, and path I have taken has never been on my own. Cindy has not just been along for the ride, she has encouraged the journey and has always said, "If it means we live in a tent, we go together." A man cannot fail with a partner such as this.

My children: They have always asked, "When will you write the book?" Well, here it is! They have believed in me and had my back through it all. I am honored to be called their father, but now, even more so, to be their friend.

Mom: What do you say about the woman who has always stood in you corner and cheered you on even when there was not much to cheer about. She has never doubted and always believed I was destined for more and has prayed this reality into my life.

Jessi Russo: When Jessi agreed to "help" with my mayoral campaign, I'm not sure she knew this would turn into a much longer journey. It is no exaggeration to say the whirlwind of my world finds calm in the storm because of the dedication and work of Jessi and the patience of her husband Jake. Jessi's commitment and excellence is on every page of this book, not because it's her job but because she believes in, and is dedicated to, our vision and mission.

Dr. Kathy Koch (pronounced Cook): My leadership and teaching path has been indelibly impacted and changed by the work and friendship of Dr. Kathy Koch. Chapter 7 would not have been possible without her wisdom and teaching. Kathy has changed my life, and I hope through the content of this book, many will search out her work and ministry. Thank you, Kathy, for being everything you are designed, called, and gifted to be.

Nena Madonia Oshman (agent): What a spark plug! She has believed in the project and pushed hard to help me get to this point. We would not be here if she had not believed and taken the chance on the Middle.

Forefront: From the first time I met Becky in Atlanta and throughout the process they have been more than a publisher. They have been a team I have been honored to compete with.

Jim Nelson: When I needed the help, you didn't waiver.

Acknowledgments

The Middle: I have met you in so many places. At times I did not hear or see you clearly, but over the past three decades I have come to respect you and honor the integral place you have held and must continue to hold in our nation's past and future. I would never claim to be your voice, but I hope I can encourage the greater use of your voice when all around you seems like it wants to marginalize and silence you.

Notes

1. Dwight D. Eisenhower, "Text of General Eisenhower's Speech on 'Middle Way,'" *New York Times*, August 21, 1952, https://www.nytimes.com/1952/08/21/archives/text-of-general-eisenhowers-speech-on-middle-way.html.

2. Eisenhower, "Text of General Eisenhower's Speech on 'Middle Way.'"

3. Eisenhower, "Text of General Eisenhower's Speech on 'Middle Way.'"

4. Eisenhower, "Text of General Eisenhower's Speech on 'Middle Way.'"

5. Eisenhower, "Text of General Eisenhower's Speech on 'Middle Way.'"

6. Eisenhower, "Text of General Eisenhower's Speech on 'Middle Way.'"

7. The American Presidency Project, "1952," UC Santa Barbara, accessed February 25, 2025, https://www.presidency.ucsb.edu/statistics/elections/1952.

8. The American Presidency Project, "1956," UC Santa Barbara, accessed February 25, 2025, https://www.presidency.ucsb.edu/statistics/elections/1956.

9. The American Presidency Project, "1956."

10. America's Founding Documents, "Declaration of Independence: A Transcription," National Archives and Records Administration, accessed April 30, 2025, https://www.archives.gov/founding-docs/declaration-transcript.

11. Romans 3:23 NIV.

Notes

12. Bureau of Economic Analysis, "BEA: Midland Ranks 2nd in US in Per Capita Personal Income by Metro Area," City of Midland, November 15, 2024, https://www.midlandtexas.gov/CivicAlerts.aspx?AID=1594.

13. US Energy Information Administration, "EIA Expects Crude Oil Production in the Permian Basin to Increase by Nearly 8% in 2024," press release, June 11, 2024, https://www.eia.gov/pressroom/releases/press555.php.

14. US Energy Information Administration, "Permian Production Forecast Growth Driven by Well Productivity, Pipeline Capacity," August 21, 2024, https://www.eia.gov/todayinenergy/detail.php?id=62884#.

15. Levi Boxwell et al., "Cross-Country Trends in Affective Polarization," NBER Working Paper No. 26669, National Bureau of Economic Research, January 2020, https://www.nber.org/system/files/working_papers/w26669/w26669.pdf.

16. Boxwell et al., "Cross-Country Trends in Affective Polarization."

17. Jeff Orlowski, dir., *The Social Dilemma*, Exposure Labs, 2020, http://netflix.com/title/81254224.

18. Sarah Pruitt, "The Founding Fathers Feared Political Factions Would Tear the Nation Apart," The History Channel, November 6, 2018, https://www.history.com/news/founding-fathers-political-parties-opinion.

19. James Madison, "Federalist No. 10: The Same Subject Continued: The Union as a Safeguard Against Domestic Faction and Insurrection," November 23, 1787, in "Federalist Papers: Primary Documents in American History," Library of Congress, accessed August 14, 2025, https://guides.loc.gov/federalist-papers/text-1-10#s-lg-box-wrapper-25493273.

20. Madison, "Federalist No. 10."

21. John Avlon, "George Washington's Farewell Warning," *Politico Magazine*, January 10, 2017, https://www.politico.com/magazine/story/2017/01/washingtons-farewell-address-warned-us-about-hyper-partisanship-214616/.

22. Thomas Jefferson, *The Writings of Thomas Jefferson*, vol. 16, ed. Albert E. Bergh and Andrew A. Lipscomb (Thomas Jefferson Memorial Association, 1903), 73.

23. Avlon, "George Washington's Farewell Warning."

24. George Washington, "Washington's Farewell Address to the People of the United States," September 19, 1796, United States Senate Historical Office, https://www.senate.gov/artandhistory/history/resources/pdf/Washingtons_Farewell_Address.pdf.

Notes

25. Stephen R. Covey, *The 3rd Alternative: Solving Life's Most Difficult Problems* (Free Press, 2011), 148.

26. Elizabeth Lesser, "Take 'the Other' to Lunch," TED Talk, December 2010, 10 min., 51 sec., https://www.ted.com/talks/elizabeth_lesser_take_the_other_to_lunch.

27. William Henry Herndon and Jesse William Weik, *Abraham Lincoln: The True Story of a Great Life*, vol. 2 (D. Appleton, 1893), 31.

28. M. E. Neely, *The Abraham Lincoln Encyclopedia* (McGraw-Hill, 1982).

29. Doris Kearns Goodwin, *Team of Rivals: The Political Genius of Abraham Lincoln* (Simon & Schuster, 2005), 132.

30. Nathaniel Rakich, "Have Americans Ever Hated Two Candidates as Much as Biden and Trump?," ABC News, April 1, 2024, https://abcnews.go.com/538/americans-hated-candidates-biden-trump/story?id=108655435.

31. Rakich, "Have Americans Ever Hated Two Candidates as Much as Biden and Trump?"

32. Rakich, "Have Americans Ever Hated Two Candidates as Much as Biden and Trump?"

33. Megan Brenan, "Biden, Congress Approval Ratings Persistently Low," Gallup, May 28, 2024, https://news.gallup.com/poll/645413/biden-congress-approval-ratings-persistently-low.aspx.

34. The American Presidency Project, "Executive Orders," UC Santa Barbara, accessed April 29, 2025, https://www.presidency.ucsb.edu/statistics/data/executive-orders.

35. Franklin D. Roosevelt, "Franklin D. Roosevelt's First Inaugural Address," March 4, 1933, National Archives and Records Administration, transcript, accessed February 4, 1995, https://catalog.archives.gov/id/197333.

36. "Biography: Lyndon B. Johnson," LBJ Library, accessed April 30, 2025, https://www.lbjlibrary.org/life-and-legacy/the-man-himself/biography.

37. Megan Brenan, "Americans' Trust in Media Remains at Trend Low," Gallup, October 14, 2024, https://news.gallup.com/poll/651977/americans-trust-media-remains-trend-low.aspx.

38. "Social Media and News Fact Sheet," Pew Research Center, updated October 16, 2024, https://www.pewresearch.org/journalism/fact-sheet/social-media-and-news-fact-sheet/.

Notes

39. Elisa Shearer et al., "Sources of Local News," Pew Research Center, May 7, 2024, https://www.pewresearch.org/journalism/2024/05/07/sources-of-local-news/.

40. OpenSecrets Staff, "Press Release: Spending on 2024 Federal Elections Projected to Exceed Previous Record," OpenSecrets News, October 8, 2024, https://www.opensecrets.org/news/2024/10/press-release-spending-2024-federal-elections-projected-exceed-previous-record-total-cost/.

41. Kevin Cool and Dave Gilson, "Pulling Back from Polarization: The Missing Middle," Insights by Stanford Business, October 19, 2022, https://www.gsb.stanford.edu/insights/pulling-back-polarization-missing-middle.

42. Cool and Gilson, "Pulling Back from Polarization."

43. Cool and Gilson, "Pulling Back from Polarization."

44. Cool and Gilson, "Pulling Back from Polarization."

45. "September 17, 1787: A Republic, If You Can Keep It," National Parks Service, updated September 22, 2023, https://www.nps.gov/articles/000/constitutionalconvention-september17.htm.

46. Paul Wallace, *The White Roots of Peace: The Iroquois Book of Life* (Friedmann, 1968), 108.

47. Seth Godin, *Tribes: We Need You to Lead Us* (Penguin, 2008), 4.

48. Godin, *Tribes*, 152.

49. Joel Achenbach, "Science Is Revealing Why American Politics Are So Intensely Polarized," *The Washington Post*, January 20, 2024, https://www.washingtonpost.com/science/2024/01/20/polarization-science-evolution-psychology/.

50. Muzafer Sherif, "Experiments in Group Conflict," *Scientific American* 195, no. 5 (November 1956): 54–58, https://doi.org/10.1038/scientificamerican1156-54.

51. Sherif, "Experiments in Group Conflict."

52. Sherif, "Experiments in Group Conflict."

53. Shanto Iyengar et al., "The Origins and Consequences of Affective Polarization in the United States," *Annual Review of Political Science* 22, no. 1 (May 11, 2019): 129–46, https://doi.org/10.1146/annurev-polisci-051117-073034.

54. Greg Lukianoff and Jonathan Haidt, *The Coddling of the American Mind: How Good Intentions and Bad Ideas Are Setting Up a Generation for Failure* (Penguin Books, 2019), 60.

Notes

55. Jim VandeHei and Mike Allen, "Behind the Curtain: America's Reality Distortion Machine," Axios, April 9, 2024, https://www.axios.com/2024/04/09/america-politics-divided-polarization-data.

56. Stephen Hawkins et al., *Hidden Tribes: A Study of America's Polarized Landscape* (More in Common, 2018), 6, https://hiddentribes.us/media/qfpekz4g/hidden_tribes_report.pdf.

57. Hawkins et al., *Hidden Tribes*.

58. Hawkins et al., *Hidden Tribes*, 4.

59. Hawkins et al., *Hidden Tribes*, 4.

60. James A. Morone, *Republic of Wrath: How American Politics Turned Tribal, from George Washington to Donald Trump* (Basic Books, 2020), 309.

61. Morone, *Republic of Wrath*.

62. Morone, *Republic of Wrath*, 304.

63. Associated Press and NORC Center for Public Affairs Research, *The March 2024 AP-NORC Center Poll*, https://apnorc.org/wp-content/uploads/2024/04/March-2024-topline-Democracy-1-1.pdf.

64. Gary Fields and Amelia Thomson-Deveaux, "Yes, We're Divided. But New AP-NORC Poll Shows Americans Still Agree on Most Core American Values," AP News, updated April 3, 2024, https://apnews.com/article/ap-poll-democracy-rights-freedoms-election-b1047da72551e-13554a3959487e5181a.

65. Ross Ramsey, "UT/TT Poll: Texas Voters Weigh in on Importance of 'Bathroom Bill,'" *The Texas Tribune*, June 19, 2017, https://www.texastribune.org/2017/06/19/uttt-poll-bathroom-bill-isnt-important-most-texas-voters/.

66. Ramsey, "UT/TT Poll."

67. Kathy Koch, *Five to Thrive: How to Determine If Your Core Needs Are Being Met (and What to Do When They're Not)* (Moody Publishers, 2020).

68. "Research Starters: US Military by the Numbers," The National WWII Museum, 2003, https://www.nationalww2museum.org/students-teachers/student-resources/research-starters/research-starters-us-military-numbers.

69. John F. Kennedy, "We Choose to Go to the Moon," September 12, 1962, Rice University, https://www.rice.edu/jfk-speech.

Notes

70. Kennedy, "We Choose to Go to the Moon."

71. Phil Harris, "Maslow, Abraham (1908–1970) and Hierarchy of Needs," *The Palgrave Encyclopedia of Interest Groups, Lobbying and Public Affairs*, 2022, 1–3, https://doi.org/10.1007/978-3-030-13895-0_171-2.

72. Pew Research Center, "Beyond Distrust: How Americans View Their Government," Pew Research Center, November 23, 2015, https://www.pewresearch.org/politics/2015/11/23/1-trust-in-government-1958-2015/.

73. Stephen R. Covey, *The 3rd Alternative: Solving Life's Most Difficult Problems* (Free Press, 2011), 43.

74. Del Quentin Wilber, "Reagan Survived an Assassination Attempt and His Response Changed the Trajectory of His Presidency," AP News, July 14, 2024, https://apnews.com/article/reagan-assassination-attempt-trump-butler-gunman-bd3c038d706de55a64727f7d15dffbc8.

75. Wilber, "Reagan Survived an Assassination Attempt."

76. Ronald Reagan, "The Diary of Ronald Reagan," April 14, 1981, The Ronald Reagan Presidential Foundation & Institute, https://www.reaganfoundation.org/ronald-reagan/white-house-diaries/diary-entry-04141981?srsltid=AfmBOoo8u8UpAg2F158_DRalhS-Ich9iEDFE91IuknYmbiCsh7vozsBw.

77. Lydia Saad, "Inflation, Immigration Rank Among Top U.S. Issue Concerns," Gallup, March 26, 2024, https://news.gallup.com/poll/642887/inflation-immigration-rank-among-top-issue-concerns.aspx.

78. Kennedy, "We Choose to Go to the Moon."

79. Mahatma Gandhi, "Seven Deadly Sins as per Mahatma Gandhi," 1990, https://www.mkgandhi.org/mgmnt.php.

80. Tricia McDermott, "Ronald Reagan Remembered," CBS News, June 6, 2004, https://www.cbsnews.com/news/ronald-reagan-remembered/.

81. Daniel A. Cox, *The State of American Friendship: Change, Challenges, and Loss* (American Enterprise Institute, 2021).

82. "A Country Divided: 10 Per Cent of American Couples Have Ended a Relationship Because of Political Differences," Wakefield Research survey report, May 10, 2017, https://wakefieldresearch.com/country-divided-10-per-cent-american-couples-ended-relationship-political-differences-third-say-consider-getting-divorce-spouse-backed-trump/.

83. "A Country Divided."

Notes

84. Daniel A. Cox, "The Class Divide in Family Dinner," survey report, The Survey Center on American Life, November 7, 2022, https://www.americansurveycenter.org/the-class-divide-in-family-dinner/.

85. Daniel P. Miller et al., "Family Meals and Child Academic and Behavioral Outcomes," *Child Development* 83, no. 6 (August 2012): 2104–20, https://doi.org/10.1111/j.1467-8624.2012.01825.x.

86. Miller et al., "Family Meals and Child Academic and Behavioral Outcomes."

87. Robert Greenleaf, "The Servant as Leader," in *Servant Leadership* (Paulist Press, 1977).

88. Larry C. Spears, "Character and Servant Leadership: Ten Characteristics of Effective, Caring Leaders," *Journal of Virtues & Leadership* 1, no. 1 (2010): 25–30.

89. Ronald Reagan, "Remarks to State and Local Republican Officials on Federalism and Aid to the Nicaraguan Democratic Resistance," March 22, 1988, Ronald Reagan Presidential Library & Museum, https://www.reaganlibrary.gov/archives/speech/remarks-state-and-local-republican-officials-federalism-and-aid-nicaraguan.

90. Newt Gingrich, "Turnover Time," *The Washington Post*, March 28, 1995, https://www.washingtonpost.com/archive/opinions/1995/03/28/turnover-time/0b84b369-5cd5-4d96-bddf-cd567727772a/.

91. Gingrich, "Turnover Time."

92. Stephen R. Covey, *The 7 Habits of Highly Effective People: Powerful Lessons in Personal Change* (Free Press, 2004), 240.

93. Margaret Chase Smith, "Declaration of Conscience," June 1, 1950, United States Senate, 2020, https://www.senate.gov/artandhistory/history/resources/pdf/SmithDeclaration.pdf.

94. Simon Sinek, "What Leaders Can Learn from Mandela's Selflessness and Sacrifice," HuffPost, December 9, 2013, https://www.huffpost.com/entry/the-loss-of-leadership_b_4414473.

95. Chris Tomlinson, "President Jimmy Carter's Strength Through Humility and Kindness Was Misunderstood as Weakness," *Houston Chronicle*, December 31, 2024, http://www.houstonchronicle.com/business/columnists/tomlinson/article/jimmy-carter-servant-leader-lessons-20007053.php.

96. David Martosko, "Land of a Million Orphans: DailyMail.com Investigates the Hidden African Crisis Driven by AIDS and Meets 'Children Raised by Children' Left Behind in Zambia," Daily Mail Online, July 9, 2019, https://www.dailymail.co.uk/news/article-7207739/LAND-MILLION-ORPHANS-hidden-AIDS-driven-African-crisis-children-raised-children.html.

97. Martosko, "Land of a Million Orphans."

98. Carrie McKean, "'It's Going to Start a Civil War': A Midland School Discards Its Confederate Name," *Texas Monthly*, October 30, 2020, https://www.texasmonthly.com/news-politics/midland-lee-high-school-confederate-name-change/.

99. Patrick Payton, "Payton: If We Had Do-Over, School Wouldn't Be Named Lee," *Midland Reporter-Telegram*, August 1, 2020, https://www.mrt.com/opinion/article/Payton-If-we-had-do-over-school-wouldn-t-be-15451987.php.

100. Payton, "Payton: If We Had a Do-Over."

101. Carlos Nogueras Ramos, "Midland School Board Votes to Restore School Name Honoring Confederate General," *Texas Tribune*, August 12, 2025.

102. Edward J. Watts, "Complacency—Not Hubris—Is What Killed the Roman Republic," Zócalo Public Square, February 26, 2019, https://www.zocalopublicsquare.org/complacency-not-hubris-killed-roman-republic/.

103. Watts, "Complacency—Not Hubris—Is What Killed the Roman Republic."

104. Watts, "Complacency—Not Hubris—Is What Killed the Roman Republic."

105. Saint Francis, "Week 11—Prayer 5: A Simple Prayer," Online Ministries, Creighton University, accessed August 17, 2025, https://onlineministries.creighton.edu/CollaborativeMinistry/p-11-prayer.html.

106. *Remember the Titans*, directed by Boaz Yakin, (Walt Disney Pictures, 2000), 00:15:30.

107. Abraham Lincoln, "The Gettysburg Address," Abraham Lincoln Presidential Library and Museum, 1995, https://presidentlincoln.illinois.gov/exhibits/online-exhibits/gettysburg-address-everett-copy/.

108. Lincoln, "Gettysburg Address."

109. John Uri, "50 Years Ago: 'Houston, We've Had a Problem,'" NASA, April 13, 2020, https://www.nasa.gov/history/50-years-ago-houston-weve-had-a-problem/.

Notes

110. Eugene F. Kranz, *Failure Is Not an Option: Mission Control from Mercury to Apollo 13 and Beyond* (Simon & Schuster, 2000), 12.

111. George W. Julian, "III," in *Reminiscences of Abraham Lincoln by Distinguished Men of His Time*, ed. Allen Thorndike Rice (William Blackwood and Sons, 1886), 57.

112. John Gramlich, "Q&A: How Pew Research Center Evaluated Americans' Trust in 30 News Sources," Pew Research Center, January 24, 2020, https://www.pewresearch.org/short-reads/2020/01/24/qa-how-pew-research-center-evaluated-americans-trust-in-30-news-sources/.

113. Martin Luther King Jr., quoted in "Dr. Martin Luther King's Visit to Cornell College," Cornell College, January 1, 2010, https://news.cornellcollege.edu/dr-martin-luther-kings-visit-to-cornell-college.html.

114. *Ted Lasso*, season 1, episode 8, "The Diamond Dogs," directed by Declan Lowney, featuring Jason Sudeikis and Anthony Head, aired August 13, 2021, Apple TV+.

115. *Ted Lasso*, "Diamond Dogs."

116. Covey, *7 Habits of Highly Effective People*.

117. Covey, *7 Habits of Highly Effective People*.

118. "Two Mayors Offer Starkly Different Views on Biden's Climate Policies," *PBS News*, January 27, 2021, transcript of episode featuring Judy Woodruff, Patrick Payton, and William Peduto, https://www.pbs.org/newshour/show/two-mayors-offer-starkly-different-views-on-bidens-climate-policies.

119. "Two Mayors Offer Starkly Different Views."

120. "Two Mayors Offer Starkly Different Views."

121. "Two Mayors Offer Starkly Different Views."

122. Gideon Rose, "How Today Is like the 1790s," Council on Foreign Relations, March 1, 2023, https://www.cfr.org/article/how-today-1790s.

123. Rose, "How Today Is like the 1790s."

124. Gideon Rose, "Why Today Is Not like the 1850s," Council on Foreign Relations, May 16, 2023, https://www.cfr.org/article/why-today-not-1850s.

125. George Washington, "Letter to the Jews of Newport," August 18, 1790, Washington Papers, 6:284–85.

Notes

126. Washington, "Letter to the Jews of Newport."

127. Washington, "Letter to the Jews of Newport."

128. Greenleaf, "Servant as Leader," 30.

129. Dwight D. Eisenhower, "Annual Message to the Congress on the State of the Union," January 9, 1959, The American Presidency Project, transcript, https://www.presidency.ucsb.edu/node/235339.

130. Theodore Roosevelt, "Address at the Sorbonne in Paris, France: 'Citizenship in a Republic,'" April 23, 1910, The American Presidency Project, transcript, https://www.presidency.ucsb.edu/node/346006.

131. John C. Maxwell, *Self-Improvement 101: What Every Leader Needs to Know* (Thomas Nelson, 2009), 36.

132. John F. Kennedy, "Inaugural Address," John F. Kennedy Presidential Library and Museum, January 20, 1961, https://www.jfklibrary.org /learn/about-jfk/ historic -speeches/inaugural-address.

133. "Declaration of Independence: A Transcription," National Archives, https://www.archives.gov/founding-docs/declaration-transcript.